IRISH CUSTOMS

IRISH CUSTOMS

Padraic O'Farrell

Gill & Macmillan

Gill & Macmillan Ltd
Hume Avenue, Park West, Dublin 12
with associated companies throughout the world
www.gillmacmillan.ie
© *The Estate of the late Padraic O'Farrell 2004*
0 7171 3595 0
Original text design by
Identikit Design Consultants, Dublin
Print origination by Carole Lynch
Printed and bound by Nørhaven Paperback A/S, Denmark

This book is typeset in 10/15 pt Adobe Garamond.

*A CIP catalogue record for this book is available
from the British Library.*

1 3 5 4 2

TO DONN AND SUSAN BARRETT

CONTENTS

PUBLISHER'S NOTE

Padraic O'Farrell died suddenly while this book was in preparation. He was, in the most literal sense, an officer and a gentleman. He had served with distinction as a colonel in the Irish army. His love of literature and drama was a constant in his life. On his retirement, he was able to dedicate himself fully to these pursuits. He was a prolific and punctilious author and a delightful companion. He died shortly after reading and approving the proofs of this book. He left everything just so, in good order, and is much missed.

INTRODUCTION

Custom reconciles us to everything.

Edmund Burke

Before Christmas some years ago, I participated in a television discussion and felt obliged to take issue with a lady who claimed that the Christmas candle burning in a window was a thing of the past. At least three houses in the small avenue in which I live, my own included, still observe the custom. And just a few months ago, I purchased a car in a midlands garage. When the deal was made and I paid over the agreed sum, the vendor handed me back a twenty-euro 'luck penny'. As the custom required, I 'dry spat' on it – hygiene disallowed the full treatment! Passing near the delightful town of Inistioge in County Kilkenny a few days later, I noticed a gaily decorated May Bush on the roadside.

This survival of some old Irish Customs poses a grammatical problem in the writing of this book. Should I use the past or the present tense? The majority of the customs outlined here are no longer widespread, yet some are still observed in certain locations. A few are quite common. For consistency, however, in most cases I use the past tense. Also, to avoid repetition in explaining certain customs, without qualification, I state what people believed.

Members of my family helped me with recollections, as well as word-processing and proofreading. Many of the customs which are recorded in this book come from my personal store of memories of things past, or were unearthed in my research for previous works. Others were contributed by many people, including Comdt P.D. O'Donnell retd, Ellie Mannix, Pat Leane, Frank O'Donnell, Denis Stritch, Kevin Downes, Sean O'Farrell, Jack Quirke, and unidentified individuals who chatted to me in pubs.

Unfortunately, the custom of good conversation is suffering in these trendy times. We are 'going down that road' with the smart set who have 'gotten' used to 'running things by' each other in their 'everyday scenario'. The 'Hi' and '2u' accompany coarse words of text messages darting through the airwaves. In the maelstrom of life 'in the fast lane', gentle customs are being replaced by a sneering disregard for wholesome living and the spiritual quest of the individual.

If some folk customs become extinct, the world will not shudder. But, customs associated with compassion, politeness and good manners are disappearing with them, making Irish society less humane, less friendly, and far less interesting.

Padraic O'Farrell, 2003

ONE

THROUGHOUT THE YEAR

In ancient Ireland husbandry and fertility were significant factors in the evolution of folk custom. Others included nature and its forces, which recognised lunar, stellar, solar movements and plant and animal reproduction cycles. People of the Irish countryside believed that angels were always present among them and that they were responsible for all good things – crops, rain, dew and so forth. Bad spirits, on the other hand, brought sickness to humans and animals and pestilence to crops.

In the Irish calendar there were two main seasons, summer and winter, which began on the eves of 1 May and 1 November. Farmers put cattle out to pasture and brought them into byres on those dates. Two of the four great pre-Christian festivals were celebrated then: *Bealtaine* (*Béal Tine*, Mouth of Fire) and Samhain, respectively. The others were Imbolg (1 February) and Lughnasa (an agrarian festival held in August).

NEW YEAR

Customs associated with the New Year are comparatively recent because before 1751 the legal year began on 25 March. In any event, 1 February (*see below*) virtually was a pastoral New Year.

31 DECEMBER, NEW YEAR'S EVE

New Year's Eve was *Oíche an Coda Mór* (Night of the Large Portion). Eating a substantial meal would keep hunger at bay for the coming year. Some areas had variations on this custom, where they made a New Year *bairín breac* (barm brack) or where neighbours flung a 'Christmas loaf' at a friend's door (*see* 5 January, *below*). A young woman who retired before midnight placed holly and ivy sprigs under her pillow and whispered:

> *Mo eidhneán glas, mo cuileann dearg,*
> *Tabhar fear a pósfaidh mé í dtaibhreamh dom*

> My ivy green, my holly red,
> Bring to my dreams the man I'll wed.

The Scottish custom crept in and, approaching midnight, families crossed hands and sang 'Auld Lang Syne'. The custom still takes place in public places, when they 'Ring out the old; ring in the new' and exchange kisses. Christ Church in Dublin has always drawn crowds to hear the bells and sing into the first hour of the new year. It is a sentimental time. Sad, perhaps, for one who looks around the circle of friends and misses the face of a loved one who had smiled back the previous year.

1 JANUARY, NEW YEAR'S DAY

Families made sure that the first person to enter
the house after midnight was dark-haired and
carried a lump of coal. In many places the same
custom was associated with 'Handsel Monday' (*see*
below) and was called the 'first footing'.
Conversely, a variation of the Handsel Monday
custom existed in western counties, when friends
requested handsels from each other.

5 JANUARY, EVE OF THE FEAST
OF THE EPIPHANY

In County Kilkenny and north County Waterford,
the *bean a' tí* baked a 'Christmas Loaf', a sort of
large barm brack. With some ceremony, she placed
it on the table, around which the family had
gathered. She then closed all doors and windows
and rammed the loaf against the entrance door
three times. Each time she called out:

> *Fógram an Ghorta: 'Tóg ort go*
> *Rí na dTurcach*
> *Ó anocht go mbliadhain ó anocht*
> *'gus anocht freisean'.*

> I give notice to Famine:
> 'Begone to the King of the Turks
> From tonight to a year from tonight
> and tonight also.'

6 JANUARY, FEAST OF THE EPIPHANY

The feast of the Epiphany, or Twelfth Night (after Christmas), was called Little Christmas or *Nollaig na mBan* (Women's Christmas). On that day the men of the house did the cooking and cleaning, allowing the women a day of rest after their hard work over the holiday season.

Around the Rossnowlagh area of County Donegal people observed a ritual almost like a séance. They placed a flat container of dried mud, sand or even animal dung on the kitchen table. This was the 'cake', and they stuck rush candles or pieces of bog oak into it and lit them. They represented family members and would fade in the order in which the individuals would die.

Children placed figures of the Three Wise Men in the family crib. They often felt sorry for the short shrift those men got. After all their travelling, they had just a few hours in the crib, because on the day after Little Christmas, people took down all the house decorations and Christmas paraphernalia, including the crib, and stored them away until the following year. The *fear a' tí* usually took the Christmas tree, after its introduction to the festivities, and sawed it up for firewood. The *bean a' tí* kept a sprig of holly to burn under the pancakes on Shrove Tuesday (*see below*).

On Little Christmas mothers rubbed the tail of a herring across the eyes of a child to give immunity against disease for the remainder of the year.

HANDSEL MONDAY

Handsel Monday fell on the first Monday in January. Relatives gave visiting children a handsel – a small gift, usually coins. They also called the gift a 'suggit' from the words uttered when handing it over: '*seo dhuit*' (here you are). Although loaning was tolerated on Handsel Monday, giving away, handsels excepted, was not. Debts were never paid on that day because if they were, many more would be incurred throughout the year.

31 JANUARY, SAINT BRIGID'S EVE

Brigit was a triune goddess of healing and smiths but particularly of fertility. There was a connection between her feast day and the coming of milk into ewes, and indeed many customs connected with the Christian saint also had to do with animals' milk. There is a theory, therefore, that a Kildare convert to Christianity became a very holy woman, took the name of the fertility goddess and became the popularly known Saint Brigid.

Whatever her origin, the Irish held Saint Brigid (c. 453–523) in such affection that they called her Mary of the Gael. She lit a fire within the convent grounds in Kildare town and it burned for six centuries, a perpetual flame of its time, symbolising the light of God. To commemorate this, along the Red Hills between Kildare town and Rathangan, it was customary to light fires on the eve of the saint's feast day.

Saint Brigid's fame lives in Counties Kildare and Louth and in localities where holy wells called after her still attract worshippers. Each one has its specific rites and customs.

The original symbol of Radio Telefís Éireann station was a Saint Brigid's cross. The cross bears influences of the pagan goddess in its sun-shaped centre and in its sunwise overlapping. The cruciform recalls the Christian saint.

Saint Brigid introduced the cross when the family of a dying chieftain sent for her to cure him. In her haste, the saint forgot to carry her personal crucifix. She brought peace to his soul by describing Christ's crucifixion, using woven rushes to make a cross. Country people continued using rushes to weave similar crosses on Saint Brigid's Eve.

In the same way that children left refreshments for Santa Claus on Christmas Eve, they also left a sheaf of corn for her cow and a wheaten cake for Brigid before retiring on Saint Brigid's Eve.

1 FEBRUARY, SAINT BRIGID'S DAY

It is no coincidence that Saint Brigid's Day was also Imbolg, an important quarter day in areas where the language was Goidelic (Irish, Scottish and Manx Gaelic.) On this Festival of Lambing farmers sacrificed a crowing cock at dawn. The chosen site was one normally associated with the Prince of Darkness, such as a river confluence, crossroads or stile.

A virgin selected from the community, preferably called Brigid, carried in her apron the Saint Brigid's crosses prepared the previous evening. Normally, she dressed in white, save for the *Brat Bhríde*, a shawl that was handed down through generations for the purpose. *Sciath Bhríde* (Brigid's Shield) and *Coróin Bhríde* (Brigid's Crown), worn on the arm and the head, were peculiar to the saint's supposed birthplace in Faughart, County Louth. Other variations included Saint Brigid's Ribbon (*Ribín Bhríde*), sometimes tied to doorknobs, and Saint Brigid's Cloak (*Bratóg Bhríde*). The virgin went to the houses in the district and knelt on a rush mat, which had been laid at each doorstep in anticipation of her arrival. As the *bean a' tí* accepted a cross, she thanked Brigid the saint, whom the donor represented. Then she left the cross in the rafters to protect the household until the following spring.

Later in the evening young 'straw men' or 'Biddy boys' accompanied the young virgin on another round of the houses. Comically dressed in maidens' clothes, they carried the *Brídeóg*, 'Biddy' or 'Biddy's Doll', a straw figure of the saint or a churn dash with a ball of hay for a head, twisted straw for arms and legs, and old rags for clothes.

In parts of Connemara and on the Aran Islands men twisted hay or straw into a *Crios Bhríde* (Saint Brigid's Belt or Girdle), which had four crosses woven into it. Young people called to a house with the *Crios Bhríde* and said to the *bean a' tí*:

> *Crios Bhríde mo chrois*
> *Crios na gceithre gcros.*
> *éiri suas, a bhean a' tí*
> *Gus gairbh trí h-uaire amach.*
> *An té rachas tré mo chrois,*
> *Go mba seacht fearr a bheith sé blíain ó iniú.*

The young men were likely to add:

> *Agus an té ná tugann pingin dúinn*
> *Go mbriseadh sé a chos.*

> Brigid's belt is mine.
> Belt of the four crosses.
> Rise up, woman of the house
> And three times go outside.
> May the person who goes through my belt
> Be seven times better a year hence.

> And may the one who does not give us
> a penny
> Break his foot.

The woman of the house stepped into the *crios* and the bearers lifted it up while she prayed. Others held it aloft for each man to step through; right shoulder first, then the head, followed by the left foot and then the right.

As each member of the family stepped into the belt they uttered an ejaculation to the saint. The men then made the *crios* longer and went to the haggard. There they held it up while a family member drove the farm animals under it, one by one.

Similar customs attached to the elaborate *Bogha Bríde* (Brigid's Bow) made in County Cork and to variations of the ritual around the country. The days often ended with a 'Biddy's Ball'.

On this first day of spring women blessed their houses, outhouses and fields with water taken from a well dedicated to Saint Brigid. Younger women would be more concerned with washing their faces in the post-dawn dew, believing it would preserve their beauty. Many young men would spot them, because it was customary to begin tilling the earth on this day. The plough could not have a guide-wheel, however, because the turning of wheels was taboo on Saint Brigid's Day. Water-mill wheels halted, carts remained unyoked and even in later years some people refused to travel by bicycle.

Fé bhrat Bhríde go raibh tú (May you be [safe] under Brigid's cloak) is a prayer uttered to people going on a journey or enduring an illness. Also, women who spun by the hearth believed that the saint invented spinning, and they greeted visitors to the house with the blessing.

Brigid was renowned for her generosity and so many households ended Saint Brigid's Day with a feast, to which they invited their labourers and, perhaps, neighbours.

2 FEBRUARY, CANDLEMAS DAY

On this day, the Feast of the Purification and of the Presentation, people brought candles to church for blessing. They would light them in the home in times of trouble and when a dying person was receiving the sacrament of Extreme Unction (*see also* 'Death, Where is Thy Sting-a-Ling-a-Ling?).

Every district had its amateur weather forecaster and it was customary to visit him at Candlemas for a prognostication to aid plans for sowing.

3 FEBRUARY, FEAST OF SAINT BLAISE

Candles blessed on 2 February were used in the blessing of throats on this day. A priest uttered a specified prayer while holding two crossed candles before the recipient's neck. Although Blaise (died *c.* 316) was an Armenian wool-comber, devotion to him was popular in Ireland, particularly among livestock farmers. They believed that praying to him, especially on his feast day, could cure ailing cattle.

13 FEBRUARY, FEAST OF SAINT MODOMNOC

Saint Modomnoc is credited with bringing bees to Ireland and beekeepers traditionally sprinkled their apiaries with holy water on this day.

14 FEBRUARY, SAINT VALENTINE'S DAY.
The remains of the saint (died *c.* 269) associated
with romance and love lie in the church of Our
Lady of Mount Carmel in Whitefriar Street,
Dublin. The custom of sending cards stems from a
time when a young swain would pronounce his
love by wearing an armband bearing the name of
the girl who held his affection. Another custom
involved placing in a hat the names of all
acquaintances to whom a person felt attracted.
He or she would draw out one name on Saint
Valentine's Eve and, on the following day, would
attempt to pay court to that person.

There is evidence, however, that the custom
has nothing whatsoever to do with the saint but
rather with the date. In the Middle Ages people
believed that birds began to mate on 14 February.

RUNAWAY SUNDAY, SUNDAY BEFORE LENT
On the Inishowen peninsula in County Donegal
the minimum period of 'walking out' (courting)
was from Heatherberry Sunday (26 July), until the
Sunday before Lent the following year or Galloping
Tuesday (*see* Shrove Tuesday, *below*).

SHROVE TUESDAY, GALLOPING
TUESDAY, PANCAKE NIGHT
The housewife threw a sprig of holly kept over
from Christmas onto the fire under the pan and

children took turns tossing the pancakes. People usually undertook some voluntary penance during Lent, so this was the last day to eat and drink well. Nobody could marry during Lent, so young couples sometimes 'galloped' (eloped) on this day if they had not parental or church approval for their marriage. Traditionally, the serious business of matchmaking began on Shrove Tuesday, so that couples would be ready to wed after Easter. In the midlands this was sometimes accompanied by youths running through villages calling out the names of couples 'in line for the banns' (*see* 'Love, Marriage and Infanthood'). This was often done in jest, perhaps pairing a confirmed old bachelor with a sprightly young woman.

ASH WEDNESDAY, PUSS WEDNESDAY

Roman Catholics still get blessed with ashes on this day. The ashes come from burning yew trees that had been blessed the previous Palm Sunday (*see below*). The priest blesses the ashes and dampens them with holy water. He or a lay minister then places his thumb in the resulting grey paste, marks a cross on the receiver's forehead, saying, 'Remember man, thou art but dust and into dust thou shalt return.' It is a salutary reminder of mortality. As a penance, people still give up some luxury on Ash Wednesday – alcoholic drink, cigarettes, sweets – and look forward to a respite on Saint Patrick's

Day and to noon on Holy Saturday when they can partake of their pleasure again.

When laws of fast and abstinence were more strict, women scrubbed all utensils used for cooking meat and put them away on Ash Wednesday. Since there would be no merrymaking for forty days, they stored away musical instruments, draughts and skittles. One rare custom involved burning the household's pack of cards on that day and purchasing a new 'deck' on Easter Saturday.

Some cruel customs were common then too. Young people sprinkled ashes from a turf fire on the backs of elderly bachelors and some spinsters. Grown-ups were even more menacing. They sometimes tied an unfortunate bachelor to a plank or stable door and dragged him through the village. In Ardmore, County Waterford, hooligans forced spinsters to dance while whirling a stone tied to a rope around their heads. At Dunmore East, in the same county, jokers waited until the day after Ash Wednesday to sprinkle salt on bachelors and spinsters. This symbolised their being cured or preserved until after Lent. A more common form of ridicule took place on the first Sunday in Lent, Chalk Sunday (*see below*).

In County Westmeath, the expression 'You'll have the ash bag chucked at you' meant that someone was unlikely to find a partner. The saying arose from a custom of tying small pouches of ashes to the coat-tails of unmarried men or women. And in the port of Waterford there was a custom whereby local pranksters tied bachelors and spinsters to a large log, which they then dragged along the quayside. Graffiti, often gross or obscene, appeared on the doors of their houses.

Tying string to door knockers, climbing a roof and stuffing the chimney with a sack, taking gates off hinges and carrying them away – these were some of the tricks played on the unwed. A recorded prank involved taking a donkey's cart asunder and reassembling it in a bachelor's kitchen while he was asleep in the bedroom. The pranksters then brought in the donkey and harnessed it to the cart. When the man arose next morning, he was terrified that the episode was the work of fairies.

This first day of Lent was often called Puss Wednesday because young women who did not get a husband during Shrove would have a 'sour puss' on them on Ash Wednesday. The Church forbade marriage 'within the forbidden degrees of kindred or from Ash Wednesday to Trinity Sunday'. (Trinity Sunday is the first Sunday after Whit Sunday.) Since wedlock could not come with sackcloth, therefore, if a ring were not tossed a yearning girl's way along with the pancake, she had a dreary, penitential seven weeks to go before she could marry – unless she went to the Skelligs (*see* Lent, *below*).

LENT

Lent is a period of forty days, lasting from Ash
Wednesday to Holy Saturday. It commemorates
Jesus fasting in the wilderness.

A community of monks lived on the Skellig
Michael (*Sceilig Mhichíl*) off the coast of County
Kerry from the sixth to the eleventh centuries.
Going to the Skelligs could result in receiving a
special dispensation from these monks to marry
during Lent. Even after their departure young
couples who had not 'tied the knot' before Shrove
made pilgrimages during the first weeks of Lent.
Locals set tar barrels alight to illuminate the way
across the rocky approach and women recited
prayers. The quaint custom deteriorated however.
Wild parties, with drinking, dancing and assorted
shenanigans got so out of hand that clergy banned
the custom (and we thought cider parties and
barbecues were modern and 'cool'!).

Before the nineteenth century there was a
Black Fast during Lent, which applied to every day
of the week and demanded abstinence from meat,
fish, poultry or dairy products. Then came
formalised Precepts of the Church, which laid
down clear instructions.

The law of fasting allowed one full meal and
two collations each day and all those over seven
years of age were obliged to comply. One collation
could amount to two ounces of food, the other

eight. Later, some bishops permitted a biscuit with a cup of tea or milk at night. Doctor Con Lucey of Cork was one such bishop and a bakery in the city produced a large, substantial biscuit that became known as a Connie Dodger.

All those between the ages of twenty-one and sixty who were in good health and not engaged in laborious work were bound, under the pain of mortal sin, to fast. There was no fasting on Sundays or on holy days of obligation. While meat was not allowed on any Friday during the year, in Lent it was not permitted on Wednesdays either.

FIRST SUNDAY IN LENT, CHALK SUNDAY, PUSS SUNDAY, DOMHNACH NA SMÚIT (SUNDAY OF GLOOM)

Those who did not marry before Ash Wednesday were suitably marked on Chalk Sunday. On their way to Mass, or as they knelt in church, someone would steal up behind them and chalk an X on their backs or sleeves.

SALT MONDAY

Mayo scribes marked their bachelors and spinsters on the first Monday in Lent. They too took the added liberty of shaking salt on their victims.

1 MARCH, SAINT DAVID'S DAY

People believed that if March should 'come in like the lion' it would 'go out like the lamb' and vice versa. Crows began to build their nests on 1 March and in some areas people chose this date to start building a house. Cambro-Norman influences were apparent in Naas, County Kildare, when, up to the eighteenth century, townspeople wore a leek in honour of the Welsh patron, Saint David. On one occasion a Welsh regiment was passing through and, thinking the Naas people were ridiculing them, they attacked. After receiving an explanation, however, they 'turned the current of their wrath into a flow of fellowship and alcohol' (Thomas de Burgh, JCKAS, vol. 1, no. 3, p. 184).

17 MARCH, SAINT PATRICK'S DAY

Probably echoing the pagan ritual of blood sacrifice, people once killed a black cock on Saint Patrick's Day. Less dramatic was their belief that Saint Patrick would 'turn the cold stone', which merely meant that milder weather would come after 17 March. In some areas people turned some recognised rock.

The feast day of Ireland's patron saint provided welcome relief during Lent. People wore tufts of shamrock – the men in the ribbon of their hats or behind the stud of their *caipíní* (caubeens, caps); the women on their lapels. Saint Patrick used the trefoil plant, they believed, to explain to pagan natives the mystery of the Blessed Trinity – three persons in one God. Wealthier people sported the Saint Patrick's

Cross, which they fashioned from green and white silk ribbons and laces. Like the stitches in the Aran sweater, these crosses featured patterns distinct to certain families and districts. A newly married couple placed a cross made from osiers high up on the back of the door. Each year they added another, until the crosses reached the bottom.

Children wore Saint Patrick's badges. In earlier times they took great pride in fashioning their own, each drawing a basic form of the Celtic cross on a circular piece of white paper or cloth. Later, they purchased ready-made badges, which were usually strips of green ribbon bearing a harp made from some cheap metal and painted gold. In those days too, men repaired to the local shebeen or public house after Mass to drink their *Pota Pádraic* (Saint Patrick's Pot). If their families were lucky, they returned in time to have dinner or to go to a football or hurling match. Too often, however, they remained drinking the 'pots' until it was time to 'drown the shamrock'.

Late in the evening, in shebeens and by firesides, adults – mainly male – drowned the shamrock in porter or whiskey. They placed their withered plant in the glass and when they consumed the drink, they took out the 'drowned' shamrock and tossed it over their left shoulder, calling on the saint to bestow luck. A very old Munster custom involved making a cross on a person's forehead with a piece of charred wood while urging him or her to remain loyal to the faith of Saint Patrick.

Early in the twentieth century all bars closed on the feast day. Dublin's dog show at the RDS (Royal Dublin Society) grounds in Ballsbridge attracted large numbers because it was the only place that had a drinking licence.

On Saint Patrick's Day, Irish-Americans, particularly in Boston, dined on corned beef and cabbage. Some said its popularity grew from references in a 'Jiggs and Maggie' comic strip, because the custom is not common in Ireland.

In more recent times, Saint Patrick's Day parades took place in towns and in cities. Modern parties featured smoked salmon and 'flags' – a drink representing the national tricolour that is a heady concoction.

25 MARCH, FEAST OF THE ANNUNCIATION, LADY DAY

In some areas the Lenten restrictions were lifted on the day commemorating Mary's being told she was to become the Mother of God. Lady Day occurred a few days after the vernal equinox. If it coincided with Easter Sunday, the harvest would be poor, so people took precautions by blessing the fields with holy water. On this day, pilgrims visited *Tobar Muire* (Mary's Well) near Dundalk. On their knees,

.they shuffled westward around the well before drinking from it. This, they believed, could cure ailments and forgive sin.

MOTHER'S DAY

The fourth Sunday in Lent is Mother's Day. Although the custom of sending cards and gifts is comparatively recent, that day was Mothering Sunday in the Anglican liturgy:

> Be cheerful, barren woman who does not
> bear; break out with shouting, you who have
> no birthpangs, because more numerous are
> the children of the desolate woman than of
> the one who has a husband. (Galatians 4:27)

It is called *Laetare* (Rejoice) Sunday in the western Christian Churches because the first word of the Introit for that day was '*Laetare*'. Further 'rejoicing' by temporary relaxation of Lenten mortification earned it the name Refreshment Sunday in certain disciplines.

PEA SUNDAY, PASSION SUNDAY

Some families of Cambro-Norman settlers observed a Welsh custom on Passion Sunday, the fifth Sunday in Lent. They steeped peas in cider, then roasted them. Then they took them to a holy well, drank from its waters and ate the peas.

PALM SUNDAY

Priests blessed yew or palm and distributed it at
Mass on Palm Sunday. People kept sprigs of it until
the following Shrove Tuesday (*see above*). They used
them to sprinkle holy water over the sick or dying,
during thunderstorms or on other perilous
occasions. Churches kept some to burn for the ashes
on Ash Wednesday (*see above*) the following year.

Older people had a saying: 'If the Palm falls
with the shamrock, then Ireland will be free.' It did.
Ireland was not free. So they amended the saying: 'If
the Palm falls with the Shamrock with the cuckoo in
the tree, then Ireland will be free.' But then:

> The cuckoo comes in April
> He sings his song in May
> The middle of June he whistles his tune
> And then he flies away.

Hold the presses on Emmet's epitaph!

GOOD FRIDAY

In Holy Week, Spy Wednesday, Holy Thursday
and Good Friday were austere days. There were no
church services but places of entertainment
remained closed. Good Friday, the day of our
Saviour's crucifixion, was a day when little work
was done in the countryside, although gardeners
often considered it lucky to sow potatoes on that
day. Some areas carried out a symbolic sowing of a

few seeds of corn. Men certainly would not use a hammer and nails, articles that nailed Jesus to the cross.

People ate their first meal at noon and remained subdued for the three hours that Jesus hung on the cross. All would suspend work in time to clean up and visit the local church. The family would go together and would 'kiss the cross' at three o'clock precisely – the time they believed Our Lord died. There were no ceremonies and certainly no Holy Communion, because they believed Jesus to be dead until Easter Sunday (nowadays there are ceremonies and Holy Communion on all days). Customs varied, parish by parish. Some took off shoes entering the church. Barefooted or shod, others visited the graves of relatives. Women wore their hair loose, symbolising mourning.

Dublin had the penance of the 'Seven Churches'. The Pro-Cathedral; Saint Andrew's, Westland Row; Saint Michael and Saint John, Blind Quay; 'Adam and Eve's' – the Church of the Immaculate Conception – Merchant's Quay; Saint Teresa's, Clarendon Street; Our Lady of Mount Carmel, Whitefriar Street, and Saint James's, James's Street, were popular choices but there were other preferred 'sets'.

On Good Friday, too, Dubliners prayed before a house (now Iveagh House, the Department of Foreign Affairs) on Stephen's Green, where they believed an imprint of a set of rosary beads appeared on a pane of glass in a particular window. The practice originated from an incident when the wealthy master of the house refused a servant girl permission to go and kiss the cross on Good Friday. She protested and he whipped a set of rosary beads from her and flung it at the window. The utterly shocked girl dropped dead and her beads appeared on Good Fridays (*see* my *Irish Ghost Stories*).

Good Friday – when men got haircuts so that they would not suffer from headaches during the following year; when housewives baked hot cross buns and soda bread and marked them with a cross; when particularly penitential people took only three sips of water and three bites of bread and nobody would move house or stay overnight in any home but their own.

EASTER SATURDAY, HOLY SATURDAY
Children became excited as midday approached on Easter Saturday. Usually, they would have given up sweets during Lent, so they would line some up on the kitchen table and watch the clock in joyful anticipation. Then, when the old 'wall-wagger' struck, they dived for their favourite confections and enjoyed eating them again.

The woman of the house set about 'marking the eggs'. First, she burned some of the yew blessed on Palm Sunday and mixed its ash with soot scraped from the chimney. When the mixture became cold she dampened her thumb and made a cross on each egg. Traditionally, she did the same with a 'clutch' of eggs and set them for hatching (in some areas, this was done on Good Friday). A *clúdóg* of eggs was a typical Easter present between country folk.

Hot cross buns and a leg of lamb were traditional Easter fare. Some households had their lamb meal after midday on Easter Saturday.

A particular custom displayed some wit. To celebrate the end of Lenten abstinence and a return to normal trading, butchers in urban areas held a Herring Funeral. They tied a kipper to a stick and walked in mock mourning to the nearest river or seashore, where they tossed it into the water. Then they tied a leg of lamb to the stick and paraded back amid great jubilation.

EASTER SUNDAY, FEAST OF THE RESURRECTION

Easter Sunday fell on the first Sunday after the first full moon after 21 March. The period of sackcloth and ashes ended, jubilation took over on Easter Sunday. It once was a common sight to see groups of Irish people climbing a local hill on Easter Sunday morning to see the sun dancing at dawn. Lazier beings looked at its reflection in water and possibly saw more imaginative choreography!

During the Easter Vigil or on Sunday morning, priests lit the Paschal Candle and blessed the oils to be used in sacraments throughout the year. Householders cherished a cinder from the fire and some of the holy water blessed on the same occasion. They took three sips of it while invoking the Blessed Trinity to ward off evil and sickness. They believed that the cinder would prevent fires in the home or farmyard.

Children competed to see who would eat the most eggs on Easter Sunday morning. They also held egg-rolling races with hard-boiled eggs. And they carried the prepared *clúdóga* to relatives or friends.

Sucking eggs through one pin-prick, or blowing, using two, was a delicate operation but necessary for obtaining complete shells for painting. Dyeing shells with water in which onions and blue or blossom of furze had been stewed gave them a matt finish, suitable for painting. In recent years, settled Germans placed decorated eggs on a tree, or on one of its branches, at Easter.

In some churches, priests read the 'Dead list' at Easter Sunday morning Masses. They also reminded parishioners of their 'Easter dues'. Some Republicans wear an 'Easter Lily', to commemorate the 1916 Easter Rebellion.

EASTER MONDAY

Once a holy day of obligation, Easter Monday
became a day of fairs, markets and merrymaking.
Blessing of stock, fields or houses with the new
Easter oils took place. Then people congregated on
hillsides for a day's fun. Egg-rolling continued. In
some northern counties, children dyed hard-boiled
eggs and often painted faces on them before
rolling.

APRIL SHOWERS

Sometimes days turn extremely cold at the
beginning of April, just when mild weather is
expected. These days are said to be 'borrowed
from March' and people call them Skinning Days,
Borrowed Days or *Laethanta na Riaihe* (Reehy
Days). It was customary to house cattle during this
spell of bad weather because an old folktale told
that the cold days at the end of March could not
kill the *Sean-bhó Riabhach* (Old Brindled Cow)
and the month borrowed the days from April to
complete its bovine assassination.

1 APRIL, APRIL FOOLS' DAY

Practical jokes associated with this day may have
come from France's *poisson d'Avril* (April fish)
or from Scotland's April Gowk (fool or cuckoo).
Some sources claim a connection with the Celtic
god of merriment, Lud.

The prankster called on a victim to look at something that was not there, to react to a warning of danger or to anything that allowed him or her to be called 'April Fool'. If the ruse did not work, the intended victim called out:

> April fool is dead and gone;
> You're the fool that carried it on.

ASCENSION THURSDAY
One old custom associated with Ascension Thursday was the blessing of tillage lands with holy water. It was a popular day for cockfighting too (*see* 'Between the Jigs and the Reels!').

23 APRIL, SAINT GEORGE'S DAY
On this day, Dublin trade guilds performed a pageant on the story of Saint George and the Dragon.

WHITSUNTIDE
Whit (White) or Pentecost Sunday, the seventh Sunday after Easter, was associated with death by drowning. There were some who would not go to sea unless the steady hand of a bride steered. Spirits of persons previously drowned returned to enlist new victims for company.

Babies born then would either kill or be killed. They might even grow up with the dreaded 'evil eye', which could cause misfortune or death by staring. A barbarous antidote involved putting a newborn chick into the infant's hand and helping it squeeze the little creature to death. A foal born at Whit would either win a race or kill a man. Children often had their heads massaged with salt to prevent their being taken by the fairies, and because of ill luck associated with the day, people avoided travelling or handling machinery.

Whit Monday was another day of patterns, rambling, roving, feasts and celebration.

30 APRIL, MAY EVE

On May Eve, the Hill of Uisneach in County Westmeath became Ireland's Fire Eye. Druids lit the Bealtaine fire, which was visible from the summits of twenty other hills forming a circle through Counties Tyrone in the north, Wicklow in the east, Clare and Galway in the west, Tipperary and Kilkenny in the south. Their fires, known as the inner ring, could be seen from further hilltops around the coast. When ignited, these formed the outer ring of fire.

People perpetuated the fire tradition with a bonfire. Dates for *Oíche Teine Chnáimh* (Bonfire Night) varied in parts of the country, but it commonly occurred on May Eve. During the preceding days, children called at houses collecting old boxes, boughs and bushes to make the pile for burning. There was rivalry between communities concerning the height of the bonfires.

At sunset people gathered around the bonfire and, after saying a few prayers, ignited it. Then they enjoyed refreshments, singing and dancing until after midnight, when they allowed the flames to die down. Later, men drove their farm animals through the embers and singed each animal's hair. The women lit rushes from the fire and went to each field, praying for a good harvest (*see also* Saint John's Eve, 23 June). Children gathered ashes to sprinkle on the doorstep of people who had refused them 'fuel'. Others spread the ashes on the step and examined them next morning with great apprehension. If they bore a footprint facing inwards, there would be a marriage in the home within a year. If it faced outward, there would be a death.

This was also Nettlemas Night, when boy pranksters hid in ditches and stung passers-by with bunches of nettles. Occasionally a girl did likewise and the man she stung was one for whom she held affection.

1 MAY, MAY DAY
May Day, when custom demanded protection against the fairies for butter, cream, cows and a host of other things upon which the little people had a particularly detrimental effect. May Day, on

the eve of which farmers drove cattle into Cooey
Bay from Devenish Island in Lower Lough Erne to
prevent their developing the dreaded cattle disease
murrain.

People gathered bunches of flowers from the
fields (some did this on May Eve) and, apart from
those kept aside to make posies to adorn the gay
May Bush, they crushed the blooms into water and
bathed the udders of cows with the mixture. This
ensured a copious milk yield. Others visited and
drank from holy wells and left flowers there.

People never lit pipes from *gríosach* on May
Day, nor did they ever take embers outdoors.

Young women sometimes went 'hunting the
snails' in the dew-dampness of a May Day
morning. Each one placed her *druchtín* on a plate
of flour. The snail's movement around the flour
outlined the name of the man who would become
her husband. They observed a similar custom on
Hallowe'en (*see* 31 October, *below*).

People in the north-east of Ireland observed a
custom something like the *Brídeóg* (*see* 1 February,
Saint Brigid's Day, *above*). They tied a May Baby –
a lavishly decorated effigy of an infant – to a pole,
while a strawboy and strawgirl (*see* Mumming,
'Between the Jigs and the Reels!') danced
suggestively alongside. Barren women tried to touch
the effigy as it passed or, if wishing to hide their
problem, joined in the dancing. They believed that

touching the strawboy's hand and stroking the girl's stomach would help them to conceive.

Before sunrise on May morning, country people cut hazel rods, out of which they carved small figures. They kept these in their stables or on their person to ward off evil. If they knew a copse that cuckoos frequented, they approached it so that they might hear the bird to their right. That was lucky, whereas hearing it to the left was not.

Giving away milk, always suspect, had further implications upon May Day (or, in some areas, May Eve, when a dying woman was once refused milk). Whoever got milk of a cow first on that day received the profit from that cow for the remainder of the year. This belief was so strong that allegedly, a court of law once ruled in favour of a man who struck down an intruder in his byre on May Day, believing him to be attempting to steal milk.

May Day was a 'gale day', when turbaries for turf-banks and half-yearly tenancies were paid.

If the much-maligned red-headed lady arrived at a house on May Day, she would not gain entry. In some areas, people painted *sliothair* gold and silver, representing the sun and moon, and gave them as presents. Urban dwellers danced around communal maypoles.

Decorating the May Bush was a universal custom but there were regional variations. West Cork people used a growing sycamore. In the west they decorated the May Bough of a particular tree. Bows, ribbons, posies, surviving Easter eggshells (*see above*) and tiny bells were common adornments.

Dublin's south-siders had their own Liberty May Bush and there was great rivalry between them and the 'Ormond' people on the north bank of the Liffey. Sometimes one side would raid the other and try to steal the bush, which would result in a street fight. Stealing a May Bush was unforgivable, however, and brought misfortune to the thief. A youth wearing a starched white shirt and colourful *crios* cut the bush, usually a large blackthorn. He was known as a Mayboy. Often, the whole community would accompany him to a place called Cullen's Wood and there would be revelry on the way back.

On May Day, too, people scattered flowers on doorsteps to welcome the Blessed Virgin into their homes. Some placed them in cow byres, in yards and along bridle paths.

Marian processions were common – lines of people reciting the Rosary while walking around a convent bower or down a village street. These took over from older customs when tradesmen and farmhands paraded with the tools of their trades.

CORPUS CHRISTI

The Thursday after Trinity Sunday was the feast of *Corpus Christi* (Body of Christ). The tradesmen's guilds in cities and towns paraded on this day. Each guild had a particular role in the elaborate pageant that followed.

In village and hamlet, it was customary to spread wild blue-jugs around the stone wall or tree stump where the local *seanchaí* sat. On this day he dressed up, because parents sent their children along to hear him tell his stories.

A very old custom called for nailing a cross of wood, rushes or straw inside the back door. When there was no more space on the door, the practice continued on rafters and in thatch.

In more recent times, urban shopkeepers decorated their windows and bedecked streets with flags and bunting. A military guard of honour escorted a robed priest bearing the Host in a monstrance. Four church stewards held a protective ornate canopy.

This day, or 28 June, was Bonfire Night for Roman Catholics in the northern counties. They tried to have theirs higher than the rival loyalist bonfires on the night of 11–12 July (*see below*).

SECOND SATURDAY IN JUNE

On this day, Orangemen in Carrickfergus, County Antrim, celebrated the arrival of the forces of William III (1650–1702) in the town on 14 June 1690.

16 JUNE, BLOOMSDAY

In his celebrated novel *Ulysses*, James Joyce describes a trip through Dublin by Leopold Bloom, an Irish Jew of Hungarian extraction, on 16 June 1904. Each year on that date Dubliners dress in period costume and walk along Bloom's route, partaking in many of the fictitious hero's activities.

BODENSTOWN SUNDAY

A commemoration to Theobald Wolfe Tone (1763–98), regarded as the Father of Irish Republicanism, takes place at his grave in Bodenstown, County Kildare, on the penultimate Sunday in June. Some political parties select other days.

23 JUNE, SAINT JOHN'S EVE

On the day before the feast of Saint John the Baptist, people gathered sprigs of the herb Saint John's wort and placed them in windows to ward off evil. They also tied sprigs from rowan trees to doorposts in stables or to masts of boats. In Limerick, children collected large leaves with strong stems of a marsh plant they called 'hocusfian'. They tapped people on the back with it, believing this would take from them any sickness or ill luck that might have been in store for them during the following year. By burning the plants in the bonfire later, they destroyed the threat.

This was another bonfire night, *Teine Féile Eoghan* (lit. Fire of John's Feast Day; *see also* May Eve, *above*). The 'Biltine', or lucky fire, was a variation found in some areas. This was really two fires between which people drove cattle to protect them against disease for the year. The oldest woman in the area shuffled through and around them on her knees. With joined hands, she prayed that pestilence would never afflict the community. In some areas young boys and girls jumped over the bonfires and the highest jumper would be the first to be married. A high-leaping farmer could ensure a higher-yielding crop. Newlyweds jumped through the flames to advance their ardour in lovemaking or to increase their fertility. The bonfires generated merriment but inevitably there would be some sad people there because it was the custom to begin migration on the following day. (Young men moved to other areas where there would be work, and many went to Scotland to help at the 'tatie hoking'.) Red embers from the fires were scattered in tillage fields before the gathering retired.

24 JUNE, SAINT JOHN'S DAY

The dew on the morning of Saint John's Day had the same properties as the dew on May Day morning (*see* May Day, *above*). Trade guilds paraded and people living by the shore took their first swim. It was fair day in many towns and some had a carnival air. Merrymakers danced around a decorated *craobh*.

28 JUNE, EVE OF THE FEAST OF SAINTS PETER AND PAUL

Sometimes called Old (or Little) Saint John's Day, a number of eastern areas chose this day for their bonfire.

1 JULY, SOMME COMMEMORATION

The anniversary of the opening of the Somme campaign in 1916 during the First World War (1914–18). In the North, the Orange Order holds church parades and wreath-laying ceremonies on this day and on the Sunday nearest to it.

SATURDAY BEFORE 12 JULY

An Orange parade takes place in Rossnowlagh, County Donegal.

11 JULY, LOYALIST BONFIRE NIGHT

In Northern Ireland, huge bonfires of wood, old furniture and other inflammable materials, which have been built in the days preceding the Eleventh Night, are finally set alight.

12 JULY, THE TWELFTH

With fervent battering of Lambeg drums, the Orange Order in Northern Ireland still celebrates the success of King William III, Prince of Orange, at the Battle of the Boyne in 1690. Marchers wear bowler hats, collarettes and sashes and carry umbrellas or swords. They carry banners of Orange Lodges. Traditional arches span the fronts of Orange Halls, the parade route, and the entrance to the 'field' of assembly.

13 JULY

The first major Royal Black Institution parade takes place in Scarva, County Down. A re-enactment of the Boyne victory (*see* 12 July, *above*) prompts great merrymaking.

15 JULY, SAINT SWITHIN'S DAY

> Saint Swithin's Day – if it should rain
> For forty days it will remain.
> Saint Swithin's Day – if it be fair
> For forty days 'twill rain no more.

Saint Swithin or Swithun (died 862) was a theologian and adviser to King Egbert of Wessex (died 839). He became Bishop of Winchester in 852 and died there. Nine years later there were plans for exhumation to remove his remains to a new cathedral on 15 July. Torrential rain and thunderstorms postponed the event and a legend began that the saint was crying about the delay.

25 JULY, SAINT JAMES'S DAY

At Kilcolgan, County Galway, a young woman arrived at the pier by boat and presented some dignitary with the 'first oyster of the season'.

LAST FRIDAY IN JULY, GARLAND FRIDAY, AOINE CHROM DUBH (CROM DUBH'S FRIDAY)

This was the Friday before Lammas and was a popular day for visiting holy wells. According to tradition, Saint Patrick blessed two bathing wells, a drinking well and an eye well at Struel, County Down, on this day (*see* 'Prayers and Piseóga').

LAST SUNDAY IN JULY, REEK SUNDAY, LAMMAS SUNDAY, GARLAND SUNDAY, BILBERRY SUNDAY, HEIGHT SUNDAY, DOMHNACH CHROM DUBH (CROM DUBH'S SUNDAY)

Saint Patrick fasted for forty days on the top of Croagh Patrick, near Murrisk, County Mayo. Early pilgrimages to its summit took place on Garland Friday (*see above*). Early in the nineteenth century it changed to the following Sunday, the last in July, *Domhnach Chrom Dubh* (*see* Pilgrimages, 'Prayers and Piseóga').

On Lammas Sunday the celebrations associated with Lammas Day, 1 August, took place in some areas.

Single girls made circular garlands from wild flowers and brought them to Mass on Garland Sunday. Families also brought them to cemeteries and laid them on the graves of relatives.

The custom of collecting bilberries was popular. It was often a group outing involving a picnic on the hill (height) where the picking was taking place.

1 AUGUST, LAMMAS DAY, FESTIVAL OF LUGHNASA

Lugh was a handsome sun god. He was the father of Cúchullain and grandson of a greatly feared Irish mythologic figure known as Balor of the Evil Eye. Lugh initiated the agrarian festival of Lughnasa in memory of his foster-mother, Tailtu. It continued as the fair of Tailteann, held at Teltown, County Meath, where tradition claimed that Tailtu was interred. In early times the festival lasted for two weeks and a day. It became Lammas through Christian influences.

There are claims that the word 'Lammas' derived from 'loaf-Mass' or it is a derivative of Lughnasa. It was a harvest festival and a quarter day.

Harvesting began and women took some crop saved early in the morning to prepare for a feast in the evening, when the hard day's work was over. Dingle Pie was a favourite in Kerry. This was made from mutton and vegetables.

Many Lammas fairs were held throughout the country. The most famous one of all was held in Ballycastle, Country Antrim, where vendors sold a type of sticky toffee called 'yellow man'. It was not held on Lammas Day at all, however, but on the last Tuesday in August.

The Lammas fairs at Larne and Altadaven were the main ones held on 1 August. On the whole, they were sheep fairs, but sideshows and merrymaking went on into the night. Matchmaking was common and, to the consternation of clergymen, some matchmakers arranged a trial marriage for the duration of the fair.

FIRST SUNDAY IN AUGUST

Farmers forced livestock into water on this day and made them swim. By doing so, the beasts would live until the following year (*see* 'Haggard, Field and Fairs').

10 AUGUST, GATHERING DAY, FEAST OF THE MARTYR SAINT LAURENCE, AONACH AN PHUIC (PUCK FAIR)

Formerly County Kerry people hunted for a wild white horse, but later they searched for a wild and preferably white *poc*, or male goat, in Macgillicuddy's Reeks. They brought the animal into Killorglin for the 'gathering' of tinkers, traders,

trick-o'-the-loop men and roisterers in preparation
for the Puck Fair. From the bridge to the square
they guided the ribbon-bedecked goat and the
crowd followed. Handlers placed the goat in a large
wooden skip and raised him high aloft to 'reign over
the fair' as King Poc for three days. A horse fair took
place in the town until traffic congestion forced the
organisers to move it to the outskirts in 2002.

11 AUGUST, AONACH AN PHUIC (PUCK FAIR)

The serious business of the fair took place on this
date, but the jubilation continued throughout.
Public houses did not close.

12 AUGUST, SCATTERING DAY, AONACH AN PHUIC (PUCK FAIR)

On this day King Poc was lowered and paraded
back to the bridge.

12 AUGUST, APPRENTICE BOYS PARADE ON DERRY'S WALLS

The Protestant Apprentice Boys of Derry originated
in 1818 to honour thirteen apprentice boys, who,
during the Siege of Derry on 7 December 1688,
boldly charged the mainguard, seized keys, rushed
to the Ferryquay Gate, raised the drawbridge and
locked the city gate against King James II (see 12
July, above). This, in spite of arrangements made

by Lieutenant Colonel Robert Lundy, the city governor, to welcome the army. Apprentice Boys paraded on Derry's Walls on 12 August each year (see 12 December). Royal Black preceptories from County Fermanagh parade to commemorate the Battle of Newtownbutler in 1688.

GARLIC SUNDAY

The second Sunday in August was Garlic Sunday and it was customary to allow horses to swim in lakes on that day. Some people believed it would keep them healthy through the winter. Some areas made this their Garland Sunday, but they spread their garlands in cornfields, believing that it would encourage the goddess of the harvest to grant a successful completion of harvesting.

15 AUGUST, FEAST OF THE ASSUMPTION OF THE BLESSED VIRGIN MARY

Féile Muire 'sa bhFomhar (lit. Festival of Mary and her Harvest) is sometimes called Marymass and is a holy day of obligation. Formerly it was a joyous occasion featuring patterns at wells called after Our Lady. Traditionally the Ancient Order of Hibernians (AOH) paraded on this date.

An important holiday, labourers often forfeited some wages rather than work on this day.

GLEANING SUNDAY

The first Sunday after 15 August was *Domhnach*

Deascán, Gleaning Sunday. Families held picnics in fields from which corn crops had been harvested, while the women of the household gleaned stray straws from the stubble. They brought the collected piles into the haggard to be used for bedding animals. Some women wove 'harvest knots' for wearing on the last Sunday of the month (*see below*). The custom was particularly common in Counties Meath and Kildare and west Wicklow.

24 AUGUST, FEAST OF SAINT BARTHOLOMEW, THE APOSTLE

It was customary to begin flailing or threshing early corn on this date. If it were not ripe, farmers spent the day preparing equipment. Should the day be windy, blame rested on *Beartlaí na Gaoithe* (Bartholomew of the Wind) wielding his flail, with which he would flatten crops still unharvested.

LAST TUESDAY IN AUGUST

The Lammas fair in Ballycastle, County Antrim, was held on this day (*see* 1 August, Lammas Day, *above*).

LAST SATURDAY IN AUGUST

This is Black Saturday in many parts of Northern Ireland, including Counties Antrim, Down, Derry and Tyrone, when Royal Black perceptory parades take place.

LAST SUNDAY IN AUGUST

On this very special Sunday most of the crops were
saved and families enjoyed a celebratory meal,
followed by merrymaking. In Counties Cork and
Kerry stampy bread was the traditional dish.

8 SEPTEMBER, BIRTHDAY OF THE BLESSED VIRGIN MARY

'*Lá Féile Muire Mór*' Great Lady Day, the Feast of
Our Lady's birthday. On this day Erris Head on
the small island of Illandavick off the County
Mayo coast reeled to the sound of music. People
made bargains and danced and he who 'took the
cake' became really famous (*see* Dancing and
Singing, 'Between the Jigs and the Reels!').

29 SEPTEMBER, MICHAELMAS DAY, FEAST OF SAINT MICHAEL THE ARCHANGEL

The holiday season in Tramore, County Waterford,
went into decline after the races of 15 August. It
had fizzled out completely by mid-September and
on Michaelmas Day business people 'went to the
sea' carrying an effigy called a Micilín (small
Michael). They paraded through the town and
tossed it into the sea. It represented the ending of
their income until the following season.

Children made chains from Michaelmas
daisies, starwort or sea asters. At Michaelmas, geese
were in their prime and so it was known as *Fomhar*

na nGéan (Goose Harvest). Some people killed and plucked geese and gave them as gifts to friends. In earlier times killing a goose or cockerel represented a sacrificial offering to Saint Michael. This stemmed from a tale that a king once choked to death on the bone of a goose. Saint Patrick restored him to life and the king ordered an annual holiday on the day this happened – Saint Michael's Day.

Others slaughtered *Cuid Mhicíll* (Saint Michael's Portion, Saint Michael's Sheep) and gave a considerable amount of the meat to the underprivileged.

1 OCTOBER
Children feared eating blackberries or other wild fruit after this date because the Devil spat on them.

5 OCTOBER
The great horse fair of Ballinasloe, County Galway took place from 5 to 9 October. Once, it was customary to hold a bare-fisted fight during the fair to decide who should be King of the Tinkers.

31 OCTOBER, OÍCHE SHAMHNA, HALLOWE'EN
Feis Samhna was one of four major pre-Christian festivals. It marked the conclusion of one pastoral year and the beginning of another. It began on *Oíche Shamhna* (Eve of *Samhain* [November]) and continued into *Lá Samhna* (November Day,

1 November). Like many other pagan rituals, Christians adapted it as a harvest festival, sometimes calling it Martinmass (Saint Martin's Mass).

Folk customs associated with this Eve of All Saints are more concerned with All Souls Day (2 November). It is a time of superstition, and of deep religious feelings for departed relatives and friends. Families hung crosses in memory of loved ones. They set a lit candle in a window facing a cemetery containing the remains of a loved one. Then they placed a lantern on the grave; nervously, because they believed they could meet up with some lost soul to whom they had done some harm. Creeping through a briar rooted at each end was a precaution against this possibility.

A peculiar custom in northern counties involved a man going to a remote glade at midnight to collect the seed of the fern. He piled thirteen pewter plates on top of one another, placing a sheet of paper or a rag between each. He shook the seed onto the top plate but it had such power on that night that it passed through to the bottom one. The collector folded up the bottom sheet of paper and kept it in his pocket. If he wished to embark on some nefarious project or if he was being sought out for an offence, it allowed him to become invisible – like the fern seed itself.

Some people made a Parshell Cross from two sticks and bound it with wheat straw. They hung it

on the kitchen wall over the entrance door,
believing it would protect them against evil spirits.
Like the Saint Brigid's Cross, they placed it in byres
too. They believed that it had to be renewed each
year, so they took the old one down and shouted
'Fonstarenheehy'.

A good fire burned in every hearth throughout
Hallowe'en and into the morning of *Lá Samhna*.
People left a little food at the door for the fairies.

If someone knocked over a candle on Hallowe'en
night, it was an ill omen, so they threw it outside.

In days gone by young women seemed to be
obsessed with getting a husband and this featured
in many Hallowe'en customs. Removing the skin
from an apple or an orange in one single peeling
was common. Tossed over the right shoulder, the
peel should form the initial of a future spouse.

A girl went to a stream that ran south, dipped
a sleeve of an old shirt in the water and let it
spread against the flow. She might then see the
outline of her man on the opposite bank but more
often she came home, lit a fire in her bedroom and
laid the sleeve down to dry. The person who turned
it would become her husband.

If this failed, she threw a ball of wool out the
window, holding the loose end. Then she began
rewinding the wool. If it did not catch on
anything, she would remain a spinster. If it did, she
would call out, 'Who will I marry?' and the answer

would be carried on the air outside. If no answer came, she went to a limekiln on the following midnight and went through the same procedure.

She might also heat solder and allow it to run onto a cold saucer to form the initial of her 'intended'. The track of a snail placed on the saucer could do the same. Furthermore, if it remained in its shell, she would marry a poor man, but if it left its shell, he would be rich. To get a good look at what was in store for her, she might sit before a mirror eating an apple. On the stroke of midnight she would see the face of the man destined to be her husband. If that did not satisfy her, she could visit the cabbage patch and, in the darkness, uproot one. If it was round, green and firm, her future husband would be hardy; if limp, he would be 'dawny' (miserable). If plenty of clay clung to its roots, her man would be wealthy. She could eat a kipper before bedtime too, but in just three bites, to dream about her future husband.

Another custom involved two beans. One bean was given a boy's name, the other his girlfriend's. A family member warmed the beans on the hearth before dropping them into a bowl of water, saying:

> Marry, marry, two fine beans.
>> In your water bowl
>> Heated by the fire
>> Will you marry-o?

If only one bean sank, the named couple would not marry. If both sank, they would be wed and have a happy life together. If the two beans floated, the couple would marry but would have a quarrelsome relationship.

A recently-wed couple sat before the fire and placed two chestnuts in the *gríosach*. If the nuts simply became charred, they would enjoy married bliss, but if they spat or burst open, there would be fireworks in their relationship. Similarly, a couple about to marry placed the two nuts touching side by side. If the nuts remained together, the couple's life would be happy, but if they moved apart, so too would the couple in later years – that is, if they went ahead with the marriage!

All family members took part in 'Ask the Saucers'. In turn, each one was blindfolded and led to the table. If he or she touched a saucer containing water, he/she would go on a sea journey during the following year. Touching salt would bring wealth, and clay would bring death. The girls longed to touch the saucer with the ring, for that would mean marriage.

Other customs that provided information on romance included: holding on to a grain of corn between the teeth; retaining a mouthful of water for a prescribed time; sticking holly sprigs bound with hemp into the ground and catching burning coals. If a visitor called, the householder gave him or her a black-handled knife for protection against the wee folk on the journey home. Most likely, however, the caller would have taken a personal precaution by sticking a pin in his or her lapel.

Traditional fare on Hallowe'en included nuts, fruit and a barm brack or apple tart containing a ring. The person who received it would marry within a year. It also contained a splinter of wood and its recipient would beat his or her partner in life. Optional extras included a bean for a sea journey, a pea for wealth and a tiny piece of cloth for poverty.

Children played games like snap apple. The competitors lined up before an apple that was suspended from the ceiling on a piece of string. With hands held behind their backs, they 'snapped' at the apple. The child who ate one to the core in the fastest time won. Diving in a tub for coins was popular, as were assorted methods of finding out about the future. People placed small piles of salt on a plate, each representing a member of the family. A pile that caved in, signified death within the year for that person.

The custom of children dressing up, wearing masks (often made from cardboard) and going 'out with the Pooka' singing songs and collecting rewards of nuts and fruit was common. The Pooka had various descriptions according to different parts of the country, but he was usually described as an ugly-looking black horse. Gradually this custom succumbed to brash commerce. It was not to accompany the Pooka that children continued the custom but with a firm intention of collecting money from householders. They even changed their approach, and instead of reciting or singing, they began demanding 'Trick or Treat', a custom imported from America. They introduced some cruel customs too; like tying a string to a knocker of an old person's house, knocking and running away before the frightened person opened up. Some went as far as tossing 'squibs', or fireworks, through letter-boxes, so destroying the innocent charm of the season.

Shaping faces from hollowed-out turnips, marrows or (more recently) pumpkins and placing a lit candle inside is popular nowadays. The smell is only as bad as the grimace!

2 NOVEMBER, ALL SOULS DAY

Many of the Hallowe'en customs associated with the dead described above (31 October) took place again on All Souls Day. Doors of homes remained open on this night – so that departed relatives might re-enter. If they did, they would discover food, drink and a lit candle on the table before a warm fire. A lit candle for each dead relative stood in a window. On the hearth, the tongs and poker were laid in the shape of a cross. Until recently there was a custom of paying a number of visits to a church. A special indulgence for the faithful departed was available if a person said some set prayers during each visit. This led to people going to a church, saying the required prayers, coming out and re-entering immediately to repeat the procedure. This often continued for hours and sometimes a sort of rivalry between devout people developed for the number of visits 'clocked up'.

SAINT MARTIN'S EVE, 10 NOVEMBER

It was unlucky to travel or even yoke a horse to a cart on this day. Women would not spin either. Men splashed the blood of newly killed cocks on the doorposts of houses and in the corners of rooms. They soaked rags in the blood and stored them in the rafters, because they could control bleeding in humans or animals. County Kerry people killed a pig or a goose and kept the blood, which had curative powers if dabbed on a sick person's forehead or on the door of his house. The blood rituals, allegedly, came from a belief that Saint Patrick bestowed a pig to every monk and nun for killing on the feast day of Martin, from whom he had received his tonsure.

SAINT MARTIN'S DAY, 11 NOVEMBER

The 'travel ban' from the previous day remained in force and the blood customs took place in some parts of the country.

31 NOVEMBER

The last night of November was said to be the
closing night of the fairies' season of revelry. People
stayed indoors because the dead would be having
their fling dancing with the fairies on the hillsides.
After drinking their wine, they got back into their
coffins until the following November.

ADVENT

Advent contained four Sundays and the Roman
Catholic Church year began on the first. An
Advent Fast similar to Lent existed in some
dioceses up to the early 1900s. Men whitewashed
their cottages, both inside and out and cleaned
chimneys, to prepare for the coming of the
newborn Infant on Christmas morning. Children
held a sort of competition as to who would say the
most Hail Marys during Advent. Scores of
hundreds were not uncommon. An Advent prayer
added to the family rosary often accompanied a
whispered petition:

> Hail and blessed be the hour and the
> moment at which the Son of God was born
> to the pure Virgin Mary at midnight in
> Bethlehem in piercing cold. At that same
> moment, vouchsafe, O Lord, to hear my
> prayer and grant my petition through the
> merits of my Lord and Saviour, Jesus
> Christ, and His Holy Mother, Amen.

8 DECEMBER, FEAST OF THE IMMACULATE CONCEPTION

This was a traditional shopping day for Christmas. Families went to the large towns or cities to 'bring home the Christmas' by purchasing gifts and goods. Some towns had turkey fairs and a *Margadh Mór* (Big Market) where everything needed for the great feast was on sale.

12 DECEMBER, OR SATURDAY NEAREST 18 DECEMBER

This was the date for the final parade of the year to mark the anniversary of the closing of the gates of Derry in 1688. A Closing of the Gates ceremony and a ritual burning of an effigy of Lieutenant Colonel Lundy took place. New Apprentice Boys were inducted and they joined established members in a parade to the Ferryquay Gate (*see* 12 August, *above*).

NEARING THE GREAT FEAST

Credit is sometimes given to King Henry II (1133–89) for introducing Christmas festivities to Ireland. In 1171 he had some success persuading Irish chieftains to swear their allegiance to the English Crown, and on finding them very agreeable, he had a huge hall built, in traditional Irish style, in a village near Dublin called Hogges. There he laid on a sumptuous feast, introducing the Irish to the customs of tournaments, Christmas plays, mumming and masking.

In more recent times Christmas turkey drives took place in pubs or, for parish fund-raising, on a bigger scale in schools. This was not a rustling of the fowl, but a card-playing competition. The games were Three Fifteens or Three Twenty-fives, with turkeys as prizes. 'Joins' took place in homes or in pubs. Men joined together to contribute to the purchase of refreshments.

Christmas cooking went on for days. The pudding was started first. The woman of the house mixed the ingredients and everybody took a turn at stirring the bowl. Even the laziest member of the family was obliged to give it at least one stir. The mother added stirs by proxy for absent members. Then she spooned the contents into a clean, greased cloth and boiled or steamed the pudding for hours. She called for help then to hang it from a brush handle balanced between two chairs. There it hung for another few hours, draining into a basin. Finally, the tallest person in the house tied the pudding to a rafter or hook in the kitchen ceiling.

Grocers gave a 'Christmas box' to each regular customer. This gift might be a long red Christmas candle or a box of biscuits or sweets. Those who spent a considerable sum received a bottle of sherry or whiskey. In return, the shopkeeper might get light farm produce – some vegetables, eggs, poultry or – God between us and all harm – *poitín*.

Turfmen brought their customers a small dray full of fuel; farmers gave bags of potatoes or vegetables. The holly, bright with red berries, or variegated, was placed around the house. A cross made from sprigs of it pinned to wood often formed the centrepiece of décor. An angel occupied each spike of a holly leaf, people believed. Mistletoe was introduced later, with its invitation to kiss beneath it. If a young woman received a kiss, she took a berry from the mistletoe. Her love would last as long as she kept it. The Christmas tree, with its bright fairy lights and decorations, came later.

A 'Wait' was a group of street singers or musicians and 'Calling the Waits' occurred in the days preceding Christmas. In slightly different forms, the custom was popular in Counties Leitrim, Mayo, Cavan, Longford and Kilkenny. The Wait wished householders seasonal greetings and accepted their hospitality or some money in return for a lively performance.

24 DECEMBER, CHRISTMAS EVE

Some of the events outlined in the previous entry were left until Christmas Eve. However, this was mainly a day for the housewife to attend to last minute preparations. Fish was a customary Christmas Eve meal. A special dish called *priail*, fish coated in white sauce, was popular. In County Wexford housewives prepared Cuttlin Puddin' from wheatmeal, fruit, spices and honey. Just like the Christmas pudding, they wrapped it in a cloth and boiled or steamed it.

After sunset, the youngest child in the house was brought along to where the Christmas candle waited in the window and it was a most touching moment when the mother guided the little one's tender hand to light the symbol of welcome for the Holy Family. It pronounced that the humble Irish home would not be found wanting, like the inn at Bethlehem. Nowadays, gaudy and expensive lighting systems decorate houses, yet they cannot compare with the sight seen from an Irish hillside in the past by children taken there by their fathers. Looking down, they saw a candle burning in every window – a gentle, yet wondrous picture.

In County Cavan youths 'called up the Christmas' by blowing notes through cow horns or bottles. Farmers fed extra food to animals and tradition claimed that the beasts received the power of speech and praised Jesus. Donkeys knelt at midnight and were not disturbed because they were recalling a night when one of their kind carried a sacred burden and later breathed on the infant to keep it warm. Some people touched the cross on the donkey's back at midnight and made a wish.

Snow on that night signifying geese being plucked in heaven; exchanging of gifts before or after Midnight Mass; 'Silent Night' and *Adeste*

Fidelis as the figure of the infant is brought in procession to the church crib – there are dozens of customs that make Christmas special. Laying the table for the Holy Family and leaving the door unlocked preceded the slice of Christmas cake and tot of whiskey for Santa Claus. The old man with the white beard took over the event in the minds of children. They had written to him at the North Pole and were expecting his arrival by reindeer and sleigh, coming down the chimney to fill their Christmas stocking with small presents. If they had been good, and if Santa could afford it, they would receive a more substantial gift.

Families devised their own customs, observing procedures, arrangements or habits that had evolved over years and that no one wished to discontinue. Because Christmas was a very special time for all.

25 DECEMBER, CHRISTMAS DAY

On Christmas Day, breakfasting by candlelight brought luck. It was unusual for people to visit other households. Despite modern brunch parties, this custom is still widely observed. Except for a Christmas Day swim by hardy souls or a bracing early morning hunt for rabbits by the men, families stayed indoors and gathered around a blazing fire. The English yule log had its Irish equivalent, *Bloc na Nollag* (Christmas block).

The best tablecloth, cutlery, crockery and glassware received a thorough polishing before the table was laid. Roast goose or turkey, spiced beef and Limerick ham were on the menu. Plum pudding and brandy sauce too. Christmas crackers were popular, if a family could afford such trivia. When the meal was served, the *fear a' tí* carved, charged his glass and called, '*Go mbeidhimís go léir beó an am seo arís*' (lit. 'May we all be alive at this time again' i.e. next Christmas).

Traditionally in County Wexford, a member of a Devereux family led the 'Kilmore Carol'. This was, in fact, a medley of carols, peculiar to the village near County Wexford's Kilmore Quay. One carol was sung on each of the twelve days of Christmas. In times long ago, however, the great feast continued until Saint Brigid's Day (1 February), when people stored away straw from the crib in the rafters as a protection against evil spirits or as a cure for ringworm.

These customs were associated with the season of Christmas before the tinsel and the paper chain, the Christmas tree and the commercial ballyhoo arrived to give us the dehumanised and de-Christianised 'Xmas'. But happily the homes of many of our country people still have the beckoning candle and the crib, and 'Holy Night' is not just an empty sound on a compact disc.

26 DECEMBER, FEAST OF SAINT STEPHEN

Saint Stephen (died *c.* AD 34) was the first martyr.
Tradition tells that soldiers were pursuing him and
that he hid in an ivy-covered tree. As the soldiers
were passing, a wren rustled the ivy. The soldiers
looked up and spotted Stephen, then took him
away and killed him. Thereafter, youths 'hunted
the wren' on Saint Stephen's Day in a cruel
practice. They searched hedgerows and when they
spotted their prey they 'pegged' stones, tin cans,
sticks or anything they could lay hands on at the
unfortunate bird. After killing it, they displayed it
on a bush before parading around the countryside
reciting a rhyme, which varied from place to place.
Here is the version used in County Kildare:

The wren, the wren, the king of all birds,
On Saint Stephen's Day, he was caught
in the furze,
Although he was little, his family was great,
Rise up, landlady, and give us a 'trate'.
I whooshed her up and I whooshed
her down
And I whooshed her into Robertstown.
I'll dip my head in a barrel of beer,
And I'll wish you all a Happy New Year.

Some traditions had a formal grouping of Wran
Boys. A 'Captain' led the troupe, carrying a

wooden sword and often riding a *láir bán* (white mare) fashioned from timber. His 'Lady' accompanied him and their 'court' always included an *amadán* (foolish man) and an *óinseach* (foolish woman). Mummers had a special Wran Day pageant too (*see* Mumming, 'Between the Jigs and the Reels!').

27 DECEMBER

On the second day after Christmas, abstaining from meat served as a preventative against fever. Usually, adults did not work on 28 December (*see below*) so if something needed urgent attention, it had to receive attention before midnight.

28 DECEMBER, FEAST OF THE HOLY INNOCENTS, CHILDERMAS

Parents called this day *Lá Crosta* (Cross Day) and believed that if it fell on a Monday, every Monday of the year would be ill-tempered or unlucky. Kevin Danagher points out in *The Year in Ireland* (Cork, 1972) that Jonathan Swift noted in his 'Directions to Servants' that 'Friday and Childermas-day are two cross days ... and it is impossible to have good luck in either of them'.

TWO

HAGGARD, FIELD AND FAIR

ANIMALS

Farmers always took care to bring milch cows into their byres on Hallowe'en and they brought other livestock into paddocks near the farmstead. Their wives sprinkled holy water to protect the animals from the wandering evil spirits and fairies that would be abroad that night.

During milking, the farmer squirted the first drop on his finger, made the Sign of the Cross on the cow's flank, and said 'God bless the cow!' A cup was kept in the stable and if a visitor called, he was offered (and expected to accept) a small drop of milk to drink, after which he would say, 'God bless the cows!'.

It was customary to examine stocks of fodder and such things on Saint Brigid's Day. Farmers used lengths of the *Crios Bhríde* (*see* 1 February, 'Throughout the Year') throughout the year for tethering livestock. They would drape one over the neck of a calving cow or on a fidgety milch cow to quieten her.

On May Day farmers drew large amounts of water from the well, because on that day water was particularly beneficial for humans and animals. In some areas they called it 'the top of the well'.

On May Day, too, the farming family and all the labourers carried tools and walked around the perimeter of the farm praying and perhaps sprinkling holy water on the fields. Some farmers blessed their families, animals and crops on the eves of all the main feast days. In Abberdorney, County Kerry, they slipped a sprig of whitethorn under a pony's bridle for the day.

At the birth of a calf the farmer called out 'God bless three times and three spits for luck', whereupon a helper would expectorate three times on the newborn beast. As the calf matured into a full grown animal its age could be determined by the number of rings on its horns and disreputable vendors filed the tips until a few rings had disappeared.

Movement of cattle or sheep from low lying winter byres or sheltered paddocks to high summer pastures was a big occasion called 'The Booley'. The name is also associated with the wooden huts that shepherds occupied when watching their flocks on remote hillsides. The Booley Sheep Fair is held each July in Hilltown, County Down.

In his *Chorographical Description of County West-Meath*, written in 1682, Sir Henry Piers quotes Virgil: '*Balantumque gregem fluvio mersare salubri*' (In the healthful flood to plunge the bleating flock). Piers was referring to the custom of driving cattle into a pool or river on the first

Sunday in August and making them swim. He condemned the practice as superstitious, adding 'this they observe as inviolable as if it were a point of religion, for they think no beast will live the whole year thro' unless they be so drenched'.

The international art of horse whispering may have originated in Ireland! Farmers sometimes tamed a young wild horse by whispering the Apostles' Creed into its left ear on a Wednesday and into its right ear on a Friday. The procedure was repeated each week until the animal was docile.

The red-hot coal, so prominent in anti-fairy warfare, was passed three times over and under a horse's body, singeing the hair in a circle around him to eject fairies from the beast. This and other treatment for horses was often carried out when a full moon first appeared in the lunar month.

When a mare foaled in a field, people looked for a sprig of clover from the spot where the young animal dropped, which they kept as a charm to ward off danger.

A man who found the iron shoe of a horse or donkey spat upon it and threw it over his right shoulder for luck. Or he might bring it home and nail it, heel upwards, on the front door of the dwelling house.

BIRDS

Meeting a lone magpie was unlucky, so it was customary to salute the bird and say *Lá breagh duit, Uasail Snag Breac* (Good day to you, Mister Magpie). A riddle about magpies asked: 'What is black and white and hops on the road like hailstones?' A rhyme about the bird went:

> One for sorrow, two for joy.
> Three for a wedding, four for a boy.
> Five for silver, six for gold.
> Seven for a secret never to be told.

Country folk would never kill a magpie. Indeed, they feared all dead birds or animals, and removed them hastily from their holding and burned them.

There were customs concerning domestic fowl too. When he was 'trying the ducks', a farmer felt the bird to see if it had laid its egg. With a modulated '*tioch, tioch, tioch*' (come, come, come), his wife called the hens to feed, while she scattered their pickings around the haggard.

BUTTER-MAKING

The sound of butter thumping around in a dash or barrel churn is seldom heard nowadays. Before churning, women plunged an iron object such as the share of a plough, a horseshoe or a nail into the milk. This could preserve it from contamination by

fairies (iron was associated with a number of
country customs). The hair of a cow pinned to the
churn's dash could help too. The lid of the dash
had crossed laths, resembling the cross of Christ,
holding it together. May Day milk was suspect and
women avoided churning on that day. On the
other hand, they made a point of churning on
Saint Brigid's Day (1 February).

Always, if a visitor called while churning was in
progress, he or she would turn a barrel churn (a
dreas) or slap a dash in a dash churn, saying '*Bail ó
Dhia ar an im*' (The blessing of God on the butter).

Happily, the macabre act of putting the hand
of a corpse into a churn of milk and stirring it nine
times, shouting 'Gather, gather, gather!' did not last
long.

HARVESTING

Neighbours coming together to help with farming
operations formed a *meitheal*. Most often, they
gathered for cutting corn, saving it and threshing.
A *meitheal bhuana* did the reaping of corn and a
meitheal mhóna attended to the turf-cutting.

In some areas the youngest girl in the family
tied the last sheaf in the harvest field, while the
meitheal called out, 'Chase the crows away from the
crop.' This sheaf was known as *An Cailleach* (The
Hag), and when threshing time came, it was never
flailed or threshed. The farmer held it aloft on the

pitchfork and his wife blessed it with holy water. In some parts the *meitheal* decked the sheaf in ribbons and brought it to the farmhouse to present it to the *bean a' tí*. If she did not reciprocate by offering refreshments, they hung it around her neck, jokingly threatening to choke her with it. In Church of Ireland harvest thanksgiving ceremonies, this sheaf formed part of the church decorations.

Not all customs concerning *An Cailleach* were benign. A disturbing ritual attached to it was known as 'Burying the Sheaf' and some claimed that it was one of the black arts practised by the wise woman Madge Moran of Meath. To kill an enemy, a man stole someone's last sheaf and spilled water on it, 'baptising' it in the name of Lucifer. Then he stabbed the sheaf with a knife before burying it. As the sheaf rotted away, so would the man's enemy, unless he could locate the sheaf, exhume it by night and burn it.

Around the Dingle peninsula in County Kerry, and in parts of Connemara, people called the end of the harvest *an clabhsúr* (the closure). They cleaned all tools and marched to the farmhouse with them, where they playfully threatened to burn them and toil no more unless the *bean a' tí* produced copious refreshments. She would, of course, be expecting their ritual and would be lavish in her hospitality. The resulting feast was known as the 'Harvest Home'.

In their hair, girls wore harvest knots made from unthreshed straw still holding grain; some men made a type of cravat from it.

Hay-saving was also a pleasant experience for all the family – if it stayed fine. Men cut the hay in long swards. When the top had dried out, they 'turned' it with a hayfork. Later still they 'tossed' it and finally piled it into 'cocks', twisting a hay rope (*súgán féir*) to tie them in place.

FAIRS

Thirteenth-century Norman bishops in Ireland received patents to hold fairs and markets in towns within their diocese. These became known as Bishops' Fairs. No summons for crime could be issued while they were in progress. Counterfeit farthings made from wood became such a nuisance, however, that a punishment was introduced to deal with fraudsters. They got their ears lopped off!

All sorts of items for the farm and home were for sale at the fair: nails, tin cans, blankets, harnesses, churns and suit lengths. Fights were a regular occurrence. Even women joined in, using a *duirling* (lit. a stony beach, but meaning here 'a stone tucked into a woollen stocking') to flail about. Tuam fair, County Galway, had two renowned female fighters, Big Biddy and Long Anne.

The Puck Fair (*see* 10–12 August, 'Throughout the Year') is probably the most

renowned fair because of the presiding King Poc.
In the past, decorated animals featured at other
fairs. For example, Cappagh White, County
Tipperary, had a white horse, and Greencastle, in
Cappawhite, County Down, had a ram. Borris
Horse Fair, in County Carlow, was a popular
meeting place for the travelling community.

The 'tangler' was important to the fair's
commerce. A farmer often relied on him to assess
the value of a beast or to search the fair for a
prospective buyer, and he received pay for his
work. He brought the buyer and seller together
and encouraged the sale, asking the pair to slap
each other's hand as a sign that a price was agreed.
A similar type, but less respected, was the 'blocker'.
He bid less than his buyer's price, hoping to make
a handsome sum for himself in the process.
Moving away while feigning no interest, calling to
'split the difference' or perhaps ridiculing what was
on offer ('I often saw more mate on a mousetrap')
– here was an actor at work. 'He might as well
have four white hooves', was a serious insult in a
horse sale, because:

> Four white hooves, send it far away.
> Three white hooves, keep it for a day.
> Two white hooves, needing lots of hay.
> One white hoof, he is bred to stay.

HIRING FAIRS

Traditionally, hiring fairs were held on the first
Sunday in May – often outside a church. This was
called *Domnach Somachán* (Sunday of the plump
youth). A man available for work stuck his pipe in
the band of his hat to indicate his availability.
When hired, he removed it. At harvest time, the
man seeking work carried his whetstone or sickle;
at sowing time, he might carry a wooden pail for
holding potatoes or grain.

ASSORTED CUSTOMS

When a farmer delivered 'loose milk' to urban folk,
he measured it into a pint container and tipped it
into the housewife's jug. Then he added another
small drop – a 'tilly for the cat', even if the
customer had none. It was a gesture of decency,
something like the 'luck penny' in a financial deal.

Before handing over a pointed instrument –
say a knife, gaff, slash-hook – a farmer always stuck
it in timber.

A farmer wishing bad luck on another did
so by standing under a wild briar and invoking
the Devil's aid.

Farmers, and even local government road-
makers, avoided cutting down a 'fairy tree' or
interfering with a 'fairy rath'.

If a *sí gaoithe* (fairy wind) blew across a farmer
going to work, he turned back.

'It was like a red rag to a bull', is a common saying, but County Kerry farmers tied a red rag to something in their cow byre, believing it kept ill luck away.

Travellers carried on a type of pawn system in which one got 'a pound boot', the loan of a pound, by leaving some article with a farmer to be redeemed later.

Some farmers chopped up sprigs of palm blessed on Palm Sunday and mixed them through grain for sowing.

FINANCE

An ancient Irish ritual guaranteed perpetual wealth. If a man were avaricious enough and knew of a meeting of three roads where a murderer was buried, he performed a black ritual there. He killed a cock and held a large sum of money in his left hand. He waited until it was dark and then, with his right hand, tossed the dead bird over his left shoulder, while invoking the assistance of Satan. Thereafter, he would never have less money than the amount he held in his hand.

For luck, it was customary to spit on money received, especially if it was a windfall in daily business or winnings from a bet or game.

THREE

HOME, SCHOOL AND VILLAGE

THE HOME

The traditional Irish cottage was a single room in width and usually had only a kitchen and a bedroom. It had a thatched roof, small windows and a half-door. In early times there was no door at all, just an entrance gap. On cold nights the occupants blocked it with straw wrapped around a pole. Inside, the hearth was the focal point. A fire burned there by day and was 'raked' at night. This involved placing a sod of turf on the remaining embers in the hearth and covering all with ashes. Next morning the ashes were brushed off and there was a small fire ready for stoking. A pit lay underneath for ashes, which was emptied when it became full but never on May Day (see Dancing and Singing, 'Between the Jigs and the Reels!'). People always left some ashes in the ash pit for crickets; they believed that some of them were hundreds of years old and that they brought luck to the household. Women cleaned the ashes with a short besom made from strong broom or heather. They used a longer 'twig' for general cleaning. A woman carried turf for the fire (and, perhaps, potatoes or other items) in her home-woven *ciseán* (basket).

Seats were often built into the sides of the hearth and visitors or passing travellers slept on a settle bed nearby. Some homes kept lodgers on a regular basis. These were often 'tanglers' (*see* Fairs, 'Haggard, Field and Fair'), *spailpíni*, pedlars or travelling medicine men. But it was unlucky to sleep in a house where an old man was married to a young woman.

In the autumn, children gathered chestnuts and stored some in the thatch above the kitchen fire, where they would harden for the game of 'conkers' the following year. They played this simple game by running a cord through the chestnut (conker) and hitting an opponent's conker.

Except when away from home, a man or woman always took an ember from the fire to light up a pipe before going outside to smoke.

The family altar usually occupied a ledge or small table covered by a white embroidered cloth. A crucifix stood centre back, flanked by statues of the Sacred Heart and the Blessed Virgin. In front or above, a small red-globed Sacred Heart lamp burned day and night, and seasonal wild flowers in a vase might also feature. Pictures of the Sacred Heart and the Blessed Virgin hung in the kitchen. Pope John XXIII (1881–1963) and John F. Kennedy (1917–63) joined them later. A print of *The Angelus* by Millet (1814–75) was another favorite. The Child of Prague statue stood on a window-sill, and a coin was placed under it to ward off poverty. If its head got knocked off, it was customary to leave it beside the statue because it was considered a lucky omen. If bad weather threatened the harvest, some people turned its face outwards, believing this could bring an improvement.

On entering a house, the greeting was '*Dia anseo, sa teach*!' (God bless all here!). Humorous people added, '... save the cat.'

Some families were thought to 'carry bad luck'. If a householder expected a visit from a member of such a family, he placed a pair of boots outside the door to ward off the ill luck. Like her husband checking farm stocks (*see* 'Haggard, Field and Fair'), the *bean a' tí*, examined her larder and replenished it on Saint Brigid's Day.

Householders would kill a clock but no other type of beetle. Legend declared that a clock tried to lead soldiers to Jesus but that a beetle witnessed the pursuit and led them in another direction.

When a woman threw out water used for washing she called '*Seachain! Hursa chughaibh an t-uisce*' (Beware! Water towards you), as a warning to fairies.

Once, people believed that sneezing could banish the soul from the body, so if a person sneezed it was customary to say '*Dia leat*' or '*God bless you*'. The custom survives:

Sneeze on a Monday, sneeze for danger.

Sneeze on a Tuesday, kiss a stranger.

Sneeze on a Wednesday, get a letter,

Sneeze on a Thursday, maybe better.

Sneeze on a Friday, that's for sorrow.

Sneeze on a Saturday, love comes tomorrow.

Sneeze not on Sunday, but pray.

People sometimes went as far as calling a priest to exorcise a home that had been deserted by a swarm of bees. They believed that the desertion presaged death.

Strangely, the heartbreak of the emigration of a family member called for an 'American wake', or a party in the home, often on the eve of the departure. The family might never see the emigrant again, so neighbours tried to distract them with music and merrymaking. Sometimes the revellers stayed all night and accompanied the departing son or daughter to the railway station or port of embarkation next morning.

Many parents still leave a silver coin under the pillow of a little one who has lost a baby tooth. They tell the child that it is a gift from the 'tooth fairy'.

THE SCHOOL

Early eighteenth-century Penal Laws prohibiting Catholic schools led to hedge schools. These were rough shelters in secluded places, where schoolmasters taught their pupils clandestinely.

When speaking Irish was forbidden, children wore a *bata scór* (lit. score stick), or tally stick, around their necks. Schoolmasters marked their 'score' by cutting a notch in the stick every time they spoke Irish. Punishment followed a certain tally.

THE VILLAGE

Men in homespuns and wide-brimmed black hats; women in black cloaks and red petticoats embellished with Tara brooches and Celtic crosses; wooden kegs of porter stacked outside bars – the Irish village, recalled in song, story and film, had a slow pace of life. The forge was a popular meeting place and members of Ireland's many underground movements congregated there to discuss their plans. Local 'trials' often took place there. To discover if a suspect were guilty of stealing, he was made to kneel while two men placed two crossed keys in a riddle. While they held this over the suspect's head, another man called out his name three times. If the man were innocent, nothing happened; if guilty, the keys moved around the riddle.

When a man met a woman, he raised his hat or cap and said '*Dia dhuith*' (God be with you). She replied, '*Dia's Muire dhuit*'.

FOUR

LOVE, MARRIAGE AND INFANTHOOD

'He loves me, he loves me not' – the custom of a young woman picking petals from a wildflower to discover if the man she desires loves her was widespread. If the romance flourished, she would probably pick a sprig of yarrow and say the verse:

> Good morrow, dear yarrow, good
> morrow to thee,
> Please help me this night my own true
> love to see.
> Show the clothes that he wears and his
> hair let me see
> And tell me right truly if he will wed me.

Festivals were held at some holy wells on May Day. Many of the people attending would be young women in search of a man. Some dropped a mug or a bottle in the well at night and returned in the morning to see if it was floating. If it was, they would receive the affections of the men they desired, but a sunken mug meant a sunken heart.

The families of an engaged couple gathered on the Festival of Lughnasa (*see* 1 August, 'Throughout the Year') and served a *bairín breac* (barm brack) similar to that used on Hallowe'en.

To ensure a lasting love, a youth brought a sprig of mint along to a meeting with his sweetheart. He held it until it became moist. He then held the young woman's hand for ten minutes, during which neither spoke.

Under the light of the first full moon of a New Year, a young woman who wished to dream about the man she would marry gathered some yarrow and tucked it into her bodice. Then she used a black-handled knife to cut three divots of earth. She put them into her left stocking, securing them with her right garter. During all this, she repeated a verse:

> Full moon shining on me
> Show my true love this night to me.
> Tell me the clothes that I should wear
> Tell me how many children I'll bear.

That night she placed the stocking along with the yarrow under her pillow, believing she would dream about her future husband. To make sure her love was reciprocated, she pulverised ten leaves of hemlock and mixed it into his food.

A gentle custom for making a proposal involved the young man presenting his beloved with freshly churned butter on a dish he had fashioned himself, preferably from oak. He did this under a tree by a millrace within sight of the turning wheel. The form of proposal was:

'O woman that I love, may you give me your soul, your heart and your body.'

A young man getting the 'cold shoulder' from his loved one would, in desperation, find a raven's feather and make it into a quill. Pricking the ring finger of his left hand, he used his blood as ink to write a petition:

> By the power of Christ brought from
> heaven, may you love me, woman. As the
> sun follows its course, may you follow me.
> Like light to the eye, meat to the hungry,
> joy to the heart, come and stay with me,
> my beloved, until death do us part.

A jealous woman who wished to forge enmity between a couple in love shook a handful of clay from a new-made grave between them. She pleaded, 'May ye hate each other like Christ hated sin or bread eaten without invoking His blessing.'

Loved ones avoided exchanging sharp instruments or gloves as presents. The former would sever the bond of friendship. And as it was customary to remove gloves before shaking hands in friendship, perhaps this explained their unacceptability as a gift.

MATCHMAKING

Romance was not always a priority in rural Ireland. The local matchmaker often decided who would be a good partner for another. He dealt with the parents of the girl, discussing her dowry and the like. Then he approached the boy's parents and set out his case. There would be coming and going as haggling about terms took place. The boy and girl might not meet until the eve of the wedding.

The custom of a woman's right to propose marriage in a leap year was known as the Lady's Privilege and has a number of variations. Some claim a woman may propose to a man on any day during a leap year; others insist that she must propose on 29 February and that the man may not refuse except by paying her a sum of money. An old story tells that Saint Brigid complained to Saint Patrick about the unfairness of the custom whereby only a man could propose marriage. She convinced Patrick, who proposed allowing women the right every seven years. But the doughty Brigid harassed him until he dropped to four years.

In County Waterford a custom still surviving is that of unmarried women hopping three times around the Metal Man, an iron monster that points to the treacherous rocks in Tramore Bay. This facilitates marriage within the year.

MARRIAGE

Marriage being forbidden during Lent, a young couple who had not 'tied the knot' before Shrove once made the pilgrimage to Skellig Michael during the first weeks of Lent, where they received a special dispensation from the monks who lived on the island (*see* Lent, 'Throughout the Year').

The priest read the marriage banns from the altar on three consecutive Sundays. These called on the faithful to come forward and declare if they knew of any impediment to a proposed marriage.

The bride never saw her groom after midnight as the wedding day began. In weddings of the distant past the bride left for the church mounted behind her father on a horse. She returned on her husband's mount. Young men who had been invited to the wedding joined in the *rás an mbuidéal* (bottle race). They galloped through fields and the first one at the church received a bottle of *poitín* or whiskey. With the advent of horse-drawn vehicles, the bride and her father left their home first in the family pony trap. Their relatives followed, and friends along the route joined the cavalcade. The groom in his family's trap came last. Sometimes, musicians played in traps or even led the procession.

Among the customs of the travellers was the marriage ceremony 'jumping the budget'. The budget was the name of the bag in which a tinsmith kept his paraphernalia. This custom was carried out as an entertainment because travellers went through the same marriage ceremony as settled folk.

After the marriage ceremony, if the groom was

a 'strong farmer' (comfortably off, reasonably wealthy), he tossed coins to children and the few beggars who would have heard about the nuptials. The wedding breakfast took place in the bride's home and on the way there the groom was held to ransom. He would be in the leading pony trap alongside his bride, and youngsters would hold a rope across the road and demand money before they allowed the party through. This was called 'roping'. As the bride entered the home, her mother broke a light cake over her daughter's head to ensure a life of plenty.

The custom of a bride wearing 'something old, something new, something borrowed, something blue' is not exclusively Irish, unlike the attendance of strawboys at a wedding. In recent times, they have become a novelty at receptions in certain parts of the country, mainly County Wexford. The origin of their presence at weddings is somewhat different, however. In less affluent times, guests attended a wedding breakfast in the bride's home after the ceremony. Most households could only afford to invite close relatives, so mischievous adventurous youths hid their features under long conical straw hats and gate-crashed the celebrations. The tradition developed and strawboys became a feature of weddings. They wove ornamentations into their hats and tucked more straw into their waistbelts before seizing musical instruments and arriving with great hilarity into the home. They were tolerated for the entertainment they provided and for one thoughtful custom: the group always included a *Sean Bhean Gáiriteach* (Laughing Old Woman) and a *Sean Fhear Saibhir* (Wealthy Old Man) and at the height of the celebrations they would, respectively, dance with the groom and bride. This would pass on to the couple long life, with a fair share of wealth and happiness.

Without money for a honeymoon, the newlyweds retired to the best room in the bride's home. This would have been scrubbed and titivated to make it as pleasing to the eye as possible. The couple's first night was inevitably marred, however, by the strawboys dancing, whooping and singing under their window. The noise and commotion would continue until dawn – or until the strawboys were unable to continue carousing.

In some parts of Munster the groom's guests assembled at the bride's home before the ceremony and the cavalcade to the church was called the 'drag'. But in this instance the groom, riding a horse with his bride-to-be on the *cúlóg* (pillion), led the way. The entertainment provided by the strawboys was called 'bacocking', because a *bacach* (lame person) in the cast provided most of the fun. If the hosts did not treat the strawboys well, they climbed the roof and covered the chimney with sacks, to smoke out the wedding party.

'Would you like to be buried with my people' was an unromantic form of proposal, but if a young bride died, it was the custom to bury her with her own people. This may have happened to avoid embarrassment in the event of the husband remarrying and burying another wife.

Sir Henry Piers (*see* 'Haggard, Field and Fair') wrote:

> In their marriages, especially in those countries where cattle abound, the parents and friends on each side meet on the side of a hill, or if the weather be cold, in some place of shelter, about midway between both dwellings; if agreement ensue, they drink the agreement bottle, as they call it, which is a bottle of good usquebaugh [whiskey] and this goes merrily round; for payment of the portion, which generally is a determinate number of cows, little care is taken; only the father or next of kin to the bride, sends to his neighbours and friends, *sub mutae vicissitudins obtentu,* and every one gives his cow or heifer, which is all one in the case, and thus the portion is quickly paid; nevertheless caution is taken from the bridegroom on the day of delivery for restitution of the cattle, in case the bride die childless within a certain day limited by

agreement, and in this case every man's own
beast is restored; thus care is taken, that no
man shall grow rich by often marriages; on
the day of bringing home, the bridegroom
and his friends ride out, and meet the bride
and her friends at the place of treaty, being
come near each other the custom was of old
to cast short darts at the company that
attended the bride, but at such distance, that
seldom any hurt ensued; yet it is not out of
the memory of man, that the lord of Hoath
[Howth] on such an occasion lost an eye;
this custom of casting darts is now obsolete.

NOWADAY NUPTIALS

If parents keep a baptismal candle (*see* Infanthood,
below) until the child becomes an adult, they light
it on the altar during the marriage ceremony. The
officiating clergyman bestows a papal blessing on
the couple and presents them with a parchment
bearing its text (the couple later frame this and
hang it in the home).

Many women make sure they will not see the
man they are to marry between midnight before
the ceremony and the time they walk down the
aisle. I remember being hustled away from my
own betrothed on the eve of our wedding. Also,
I remember drinking tea in the motor-car outside
the door of her home when we called before a

month had elapsed since the wedding day
(newlyweds never entered the bride's home until a
month had passed).

Since the arrival of the motor-car the custom of
a cavalcade from the church to the hotel where the
reception is taking place has arisen. Bedecked with
ribbons, the bride and groom's car leads and others
follow, blowing the car horns constantly. Guests
congregate around the couple and sing 'For they are
jolly good fellows', and the bride throws her
bouquet among her guests. Unmarried women rush
for it and whoever catches it will be married within
a year. Practical jokes are common: apple-pie beds,
old shoes tied to the rear fender of the car and 'Just
Married' sprayed on the boot, confetti in suitcases –
anything to embarrass the young couple!

A couple lucky enough to own a house move in
on a Friday, if possible. They avoid Saturday because
'Saturday flitting means short sitting'. The bride
prays in each corner of every room and deposits
some article of clothing there. She leaves it overnight
before tidying it away. First-time visitors always
bring a small gift but never take anything away.

As soon as possible, the couple arranges to
have the house blessed by a priest or, better still,
have a Mass said in it.

PREGNANCY

There were many customs associated with
pregnancy. Long before the introduction of

ultrasound techniques, a woman would run a needle and about two feet of thread through a cork. Holding the thread by the end, she would hold it over a pregnant friend. The cork would begin to circle in a clockwise direction if the woman was carrying a boy and anti-clockwise if it was a girl.

A pregnant woman avoided walking on a grave in the belief that this would give her child a club foot. If she did so accidentally, she knelt on the grave and prayed for the soul of the person interred. Then she removed her right shoe and made the Sign of the Cross three times on its sole. Stumbling in the cemetery while attending a funeral could cause the same disability to the child, unless a friend threw some earth from a grave at the woman.

If a pregnant woman came upon a hare, she tore the hem of her petticoat. Doing so ensured that her baby would not have a harelip.

INFANTHOOD

If a woman gave birth to a son on Good Friday, she usually asked that he be baptised with the newly blessed oils on Easter Sunday, something that would give the gift of healing. Additionally, if that child grew up and happened to die on Easter Sunday, he would gain immediate admission to heaven.

If an infant died during birth, the mourners never nailed down the lid of its coffin. Doing so would mean that its mother would never have another child.

A woman who had attended a wake dipped her hands in holy water before handling an infant.

The moment of birth had to take place when all the presses (cabinets) in the house were open. As soon as the child was delivered, these were locked. This would prevent the fairies from getting in to hide, awaiting their chance to steal the baby.

Difficult confinements called for the presence of a seventh son, who would shake the patient three times. If a seventh son were not readily available, any man who was not married to a red-haired woman would do. Most effective of all, however, was a drink of milk into which the black powder from six heads of blasted barley had been mixed.

On first seeing his baby, a new father kissed it five times, but everybody made the Sign of the Cross over it before taking it into their arms. The requirement ended as soon as the infant was baptised.

In the past, baptism took place quickly. People dreaded the possibility of the child dying without having received the sacrament. Regarding baptism, the catechism taught: 'In case of necessity, any lay man or woman can give it.' And they did, in cases of miscarriage, still birth or accident at birth. A helpful woman sewed a tiny piece of metal into the hem of some article of the baby's clothing until it was baptised. Nobody would remove a coal of fire from the house until after the event either. People never threw water out of the house until after a child was christened.

Parents kept the baptismal candle of each child and lit it on the family altar on the anniversary of the christening and, sometimes, on the child's birthday. They also lit it on the days the child made its first confession, received first Holy Communion and at its Confirmation ceremony (*see also* Marriage, *above*). Whether the family was poor or rich, it was customary to present a christening mug, bowl or spoon to a child. Depending on the donor's means, these could be made from earthenware, pewter or silver.

Ghoulish customs existed for babies born at Whitsuntide, for a baby born at that time would either kill or be killed (for antidote, *see* Whitsuntide, 'Throughout the Year'). Some families dug a small grave and momentarily laid the infant in it to avert the disaster.

Friends seeing a baby for the first time placed a handsel, usually a coin, under its pillow.

The 'churching' of a mother took place after the birth. She went to a church to thank God for the favour of having given birth. She held a lighted candle and a priest blessed her and recited Psalm 24 and other prayers.

FIVE

PRAYERS AND PISEÓGA

HOLY WELLS

From beside some wells people thought it lucky to observe a rising sun, particularly on Easter Sunday morning. Such a well was called a Sunday's Well.

People who had been cured or assisted by the intercession of the saint associated with the holy well often left mementos. These crutches, rosary beads, pieces of bandage and assorted rags are still seen on bushes and trees around these wells. A gaudily dressed woman was often described as being like 'a bush at a holy well'.

'Paying rounds' was an accepted ritual at many holy wells. The pilgrim walked around the well in a sunwise direction, drank its waters and scraped a cross on a stone from the well with another sharp-edged stone.

A holy well would dry up if desecrated, it was thought, but its curative powers would then be transferred to a nearby tree. People could stick pins into the tree where previously they drank the well water, or hammer coins into it.

Eye wells cured sight loss or eye infections. Some cured sight deficiencies in animals – but at the risk of the owner becoming infected. (*See also*

Patterns, 'Between the Jigs and the Reels!'. Cures
from holy wells are treated fully in my other
volume *Irish Folk Cures* in this Gill & Macmillan
series.)

MASS

Mass rocks are common throughout Ireland. Priests
used them as altars for celebrating the Sacrifice
when Penal Laws banned it. It was customary to
place a lookout on a nearby hill to warn the priest
and congregation of approaching danger. Later,
schoolmasters trained young boys to 'serve Mass',
and learn its Latin responses. A boy's first day in
this role was important and was usually followed
by some minor celebration. At Mass, men knelt on
one side of the church, women on the other. A
latecomer threw his cap down on the floor of the
porch and knelt down on one knee. There is still
an annual Dockers' Mass in Dolan's public house
in Dock Road, Limerick city – despite the fact that
in times long past the premises, allegedly, was a
brothel. Kilkenny had its 'One o'clock in the
Brewery', a late Sunday Mass, popular with
Saturday night boozers.

STATIONS

House stations took place in March and October
(and still do in some areas). The owners of the
selected house scrubbed and painted their premises

and often fitted new curtains and even furnishings. They may have wished to impress neighbours who would be attending, but many of greater faith believed they were preparing the home for God's visit. In some areas the same house was used for generations – twice per year for over a hundred years perhaps. Members of the family who were living abroad often came home for 'The Station'. The priest arrived to hear confessions before Mass. Family members served Mass and there was a meal afterwards. The man of the house sat at the head of the table with the priest at his right hand. Other men sat, too, but in early times no woman did so. The woman of the house, helped by her daughters and close female friends, served the men. Afterwards, if it was fine, the men went into the yard to smoke and chat, while the women cleaned up. Then all assembled inside again and perhaps had a few drinks. Women's liberation had not arrived in rural Ireland then!

PILGRIMAGES

Croagh Patrick

A collection of physical features commemorating Saint Patrick brought pilgrims to the Westport–Louisburgh area of County Mayo. These included *Dabhach Phádraigh* (Patrick's Tub), *Tóchar Phádraigh* (Patrick's Causeway), *Tobar na nDeochanna* (Well of the Drinks), *Teampaill na bhFiacal* (Church of the Teeth) and *Leaba Phádraigh* (Saint Patrick's Bed). The pilgrimage to Croagh Patrick involved a dawn (sometimes even a pre-dawn) ascent from Murrisk (*see* Last Sunday in July, Reek Sunday, 'Throughout the Year'), where pedlars sold ash plants to assist the climbers and cups of tea to thirsty travellers. Then, barefooted, the pilgrims began the *turas* (journey). Sharp stones were a hazard, especially on the final *cruach* (pile). At its base was *Leacht Mhionnáin* (Saint Benignus's Memorial [mound]). This was the location of the first station of the pilgrimage. It involved prayer recital during seven *deisil* (sunwise circuits).

Up the *Casán Phádraig* (Patrick's Path) then to *Teampaill Phádraigh* (Patrick's Church) on the summit. The celebration of Mass here is customary nowadays but the old penitential rite of fifteen *deisil* around the summit survives. Prayers at another *Leaba Phádraig*, followed by seven *deisil* around it, preceded the final station. This was at three mounds of stones known as *An Garraí Mór* (The Big Garden) or *Roilig Mhuire* (Mary's Graveyard). A staggering seven *deisil* around each mound and seven more around the group left pilgrims weary as they faced the hazardous descent. Some hardy souls then continued on to *Log na nDeamhan*, near Kilgeever, beneath which the famous serpents that the saint banished from the mountain are said to lie.

Lough Derg

There was an early reference to 'Saint Patrick's Purgatory' in 1184 (*Tractatus de Purgatorio Sancti Patricii* by Henry of Saltre), and *Traits and Stories of the Irish Peasantry* by William Carleton (1794–1869) includes a story describing the Lough Derg pilgrim. Station Island in the County Donegal lake had a cave that the early Christians believed was the gateway to hell, from which the saint expelled the snakes and demons from Ireland. In 1497 Pope Alexander VI condemned pilgrimages to the island and Oliver Cromwell (1599–1658) later destroyed its church, but Christians continued to undergo its penitential rigours, which include walking barefoot around six penitential beds, the remains of monks' cells, reciting prescribed prayers. Standing with outstretched arms and denouncing the world, the flesh and the Devil, keeping an all-night vigil, and fasting for three days are also difficult. Until comparatively recently only 'Lough Derg Soup' (hot water, salt and pepper) was allowed as refreshment. 'Meals' of black tea and cold, dry toast were then added.

Families have 'done Lough Derg' for years, handing down the custom through generations. Atoning for past sins, praying for success in examinations, and the salvation of relatives' souls are among the most common intentions among pilgrims nowadays.

Saul

Saint Patrick built his first chapel at Saul (*Sabhall Pádraic*, Patrick's Barn), near Downpatrick, County Down. Four wells named after him are situated in Struel close by, fed by a common source under Saint Patrick's Chair. Believers visited the wells on *Crom Dubh's* Friday, the Friday before Lammas (*see* 'Throughout the Year'). Working from the most northern well, they drank from the first, rubbed waters from the second on sore eyes, doused ailing limbs with water from the third and blessed other affected areas with waters from the fourth. The place became a spa, with men's and women's bath houses, and there was an annual pilgrimage on Saint John's Eve (23 June).

Knock

Pilgrimages to Knock, where the Blessed Virgin is said to have appeared in 1879, are popular too.

The Family Rosary

The custom of the family Rosary prevailed in Irish Catholic homes until the mid-twentieth century. Each household member's set of rosary beads was kept in a nook beside the hearth and at a certain time, usually after the evening meal, all pulled out a chair or stool and knelt before it, arms leaning on its seat. It was customary for the mother to 'give out the Rosary' and intone its first mystery. In order of seniority then – father, eldest child and so on to the youngest – each member 'gave out a decade', saying the first half of the Our Father and each of the ten Hail Marys. Young children occasionally started to giggle and others took it up until the mother reprimanded them.

Members of less robust faith than the mother's often endured the five mysteries but baulked at the woman's 'trimmins'. These trimmings, or extra prayers for special intention, sometimes took as long as the Rosary itself.

PRAYERS AND PRACTICES

Arguably, Ireland's best-known custom is the ringing of the Angelus bell at noon and at six o'clock in the evening. Religious communities also ring it at six o'clock in the morning. The name comes from the first word in the Latin version of the prayer that accompanies the ringing, 'Angelus Domini' ([The] Angel of the Lord). There are three sets of three chimes, followed by nine chimes. The custom originated when monks in early monasteries called the faithful in the surrounding countryside to pray along with them.

No matter how humble the fare, every Irish mother 'gave out the grace' before meals:

Blessed, O Lord, and these Thy gifts
Which of Thy bounty we are about to receive
Through Christ Our Lord, Amen.

Some families said grace with her; others just joined in at the end with 'Amen'.

Before going to bed, people prayed:

> There are four corners on my bed
> And over them four angels spread.
> Matthew, Mark, Luke and John
> God bless the bed that I lie on.

Last thing before going to sleep, they made the Sign of the Cross on their lips with their thumb and uttered the word 'Jesus', so that, if they died in their sleep, the last word uttered was their Saviour's name. They went to sleep with arms crossed over breasts, in memory of Christ's cross.

On hearing a clock strike the hour, people prayed:

> Jesus, this hour I give to Thee
> For all the past hour, pardon me.
> I know that I shall soon depart
> So hide me in Thy Sacred Heart.

People crossed themselves passing a church, saying, 'In the name of the Father and of the Son and of the Holy Ghost [now Holy Spirit]'. Similarly, when passing a cemetery, they crossed themselves, saying, 'The Lord have mercy on them'. If any of their relatives were buried there, they prayed especially for

the repose of their souls. The 'Croppy Boy' of the
1798 United Irishmen rebellion ballad thought that
neglecting to do so was sinful and told his confessor:

> When passing a churchyard one day in haste
> I forgot to pray for my mother's rest.

Sick people blessed themselves with relics of saints, a
custom that survives. They had great faith in certain
saints for particular diseases, e.g. Saints Rita and
Perigrene for cancer. Devotion to Saint Theresa (the
Little Flower), Saint Padre Pio and Saint Martin de
Porres became popular. People called on Saint
Anthony to find something they had lost, promising
to put money in one of his shrines if they found it.
A ringing in the ear, called a 'bell in the ear', was a
suffering soul in purgatory appealing for a prayer.
Tinitus sufferers must have prayed hard!

The Presbyterian Church allowed only
communicants to vote at congregational meetings.
Therefore, members received a metal token (later
card) from elders a week or so before a Holy
Communion service. They handed it in when they
took the bread and their names were entered in the
Communion roll book.

PISEÓGA

Superstitious customs have been covered in
a number of publications, including Dáithí

Ó hÓgáin's *Irish Superstitions* in this Gill &
Macmillan series and my own *Superstitions of the
Irish Country People* (Dublin & Cork, 1978).

People carried a four-leafed clover for good
luck.

After yawning, a person made the Sign of the
Cross on the lips with the thumb. This barred
entry of evil spirits.

To prevent bad luck following a person who spilt
salt, he or she threw a pinch of it over the shoulder.

Often for a dare, a Dubliner walked twice
around the 'Black Church' because by doing so he
could meet the Devil! This former Church of Ireland
building, Saint Mary's Chapel-of-Ease in Saint
Mary's Place, got its nickname because of the black
calp used in its construction. Austin Clarke
(1896–1974) entitled one volume of autobiography
Twice Round the Black Church (1962).

A *sí gaoithe* (fairy wind) was a sudden
whirlwind lasting just a few seconds. It was also
known as a *poc sí* (fairy stroke). When it occurred,
fairies were launching a sudden assault, throwing
darts. Humans crossed themselves and sometimes
ran in a circle, sunwise, to avert danger. Friends
dipped some pointed instrument into water and
the witness to the wind drank it.

Saints Island in the River Shannon held ruins
of a monastery whose monks left a Swearing Stone,
a lie detector of its time. Accusers brought a

suspected criminal to this place. If he lied, the stone would project a mark on his forehead that would pass down through several generations. A parent ordered a child suspected of lying, 'Put out your tongue and see if there's a black mark on it.'

Nobody discussed a dream until after breakfast and it was preferable to tell about it first to a girl named Mary.

People studied *Old Moore's Almanac* for the phases of the moon and always went outside to view a new moon and bow to it. They believed that seeing it through glass was unlucky. A popular song advised: 'Turn the money in your pocket, whenever you see a new moon.' On seeing one in bygone days, a person dropped on his knees and said an Our Father and Hail Mary for some favour received.

SIX

THE SEA

Fishing folk have enormous respect for the sea and while old customs have for the most part disappeared, they linger on among remote seafaring communities. Persons drowned at sea were buried below the tidemark if brought ashore but there was a certain reluctance to reclaim a body from the sea; recovery could anger the waves into claiming another life in its stead. Attempts to find the body of a drowned person were always traumatic. In some areas the searchers lit a candle and set it on a sheaf of corn before placing it on the water. They believed it would float until it located the body, when it would stop.

Fishermen always boarded a boat from the port side, even if its positioning made this difficult. Women threw a burning ember after a departing craft, believing it would keep its crew safe. In some areas they threw it after a fisherman when he was leaving the house to go to sea.

The spring tide closest to Saint Brigid's Day was called *Rabharta na Féile Bríde*. Fishermen did not go to sea on that day but gathered seaweed and collected shellfish on the shore. Some placed a cockle in each corner of the house to ensure good fishing and a bountiful table during the following year. The spring tide closest to the spring equinox was called *Rabharta mór an Earraigh na Féile Pádraic na néan* (lit. the tide of the spring of Saint Patrick's Day of the Birds). Autumn's (Michaelmas) equivalent was *Rabharta mór an Fhómhair, na Féile Michíl* (*see* 29 September, 'Throughout the Year'). Saint John's Day (24 June) was important for the fishing community and priests blessed nets and boats on that day (*see* The Claddagh, *below*).

Some fishing families used oils from the livers of halibut, ling and cod as a substitute for forbidden dairy products like butter during Lent. If the plants called 'flaggers' were in bloom in May, sea folk used them to decorate their May Bush. They also brought bunches of them on board.

Fishermen had a custom of lashing three boats together when leaving a harbour, because it was unlucky to be the third boat out. Bad luck followed taking a short-cut from established routes near the shore. Cleaning a boat thoroughly was said to be unlucky, as was the cleaning of sea-boots before the end of the fishing season.

If a fisherman wanted a smoke and asked a crew member for a match, he never received a full match. The donor split it in two – not out of miserliness but to avoid giving away luck. Crew members brought along their own drinking water, because, again, it was unlucky to part with some. The skipper always brought a knife on board for tossing into the sea if a storm arose. If he needed the knife for any other purpose, he stuck it in the mast before passing it on to one of the crew. When not in use, however, it was unlucky to stick the knife in the mast. While on board, men never referred to a pig and were wary of rats and weasels.

A religious people, seafarers had a particularly strong devotion to the Mother of God. They often made a small altar featuring her statue under the main mast. Boats remained tied up in harbours on Good Friday.

If a fisherman married, it was customary for the groom to 'treat the fleet' in a decorated boat with his bride at the helm. This, seafarers believed, would make the craft safe against the most severe storms or swells. (On other days, it was unlucky to have a woman on board.)

Granite stones were never used to weigh down nets, nor were nets ever loaded onto a craft on an ebb tide.

Some customs of the sea were peculiar. For instance, few fishermen ever learned to swim. They tied crosses made from straw and flowers to their doorposts on Saint Patrick's Day. Some killed a black cock. On Saint Michael's Day, 29 September, they killed a goose and feasted on it.

AROUND THE COAST AND A LITTLE INLAND
The salmon fishermen of the River Bush in Antrim held their Salmon Dinner, the most important

social event of the year. Either at the start of the season in June, or at the end of it in September, they feasted on salmon chowder, salmon steaks and washed it all down with water from Saint Columb's Rill, a tributary of the Bush. The fine water rose in peaty soil and flowed over basalt rock. Before drinking it, of course, it was suitably treated and distilled as Old Bushmills whiskey!

Along the north-west coastline some of the catch was always left on board. On the outward journey, County Donegal fishermen turned their backs to the shore and prayed. When they reached the fishing ground, they recited all fifteen decades of the Rosary, as well as the Litany of the Blessed Virgin. Wives of fishermen in Teelin prayed at *Tobar na Corach* (Well of the Fish Weir), also called the Well of the Favourable Wind. If it were not raining when the tide was covering a certain sandbank there, it would remain fine for a day. Teelin fishermen would never lose their nets in a dangerous sea as long as they tied a piece of *bratóg* to them. This was a piece of cloth from the *Bratóg Bhríde* (Saint Brigid's Cloak, *see* 1 February, 'Throughout the Year').

Journeymen and sailors carried clay from Saint Mogue's Island on the River Erne in County Cavan for protection against accident or storm.

On Inisheer, one of the Aran Islands off the County Galway coast, the tiny church of Saint Chaomhain fills up with sand blown from the shore and it was customary on 14 June to clear the sand from the building, light candles and pray. Allegedly, the ritual once cured a lame man.

The Lord Mayor of Cork was also Admiral of the city's harbour. He and the Corporation stipulated their authority by sailing to the mouth of the harbour on 1 August each year and casting a harpoon or dart into the waters.

Few County Wexford fishermen have put to sea on Saint Martin's Eve (10 November) since seventy crewmen lost their lives on 10 November 1762. Tradition states that they refused to heed a warning of impending danger given by the saint who appeared on the sea. Others had reservations about fishing on 19 December, because on that date the Fayth fishing fleet was lost in 1833.

On the east coast, the crew left boats in harbour lying towards the quay wall on Good Friday. They welcomed wet weather as a sign of empathy with Christ's death. 'Shore food' or shellfish was their diet for the day and they trimmed their toenails and fingernails.

County Wicklow fishermen always put to sea in a sunwise direction and all fishermen liked to turn a boat towards the sun or to the right.

THE CLADDAGH

You will sit and watch the moon rise
over Claddagh
Or see the sun going down on Galway Bay.

The Claddagh was a compact group of thatched cottages in Galway, the homes of local fishermen. In some form, it existed as far back as the fifth century. The dwellings still survive, but with modern slated or tiled roofs. Over every door in the old Claddagh there was a mosaic of the Sacred Heart. The community elected one householder as King of the Claddagh each year on Saint John's Day (24 June). They elected a mayor and sheriff too. Then the whole community walked in procession through Galway, led by men carrying poles with bales of reeds tied to them. That night, they burned the reeds in the midst of great merrymaking. In more recent times, a very colourful ceremony took place annually in the Claddagh. Skippers adorned their boats with bunting and the priest invoked the blessing of the Holy Trinity.

The Claddagh ring depicts two hands holding a crowned heart. It was based on the Italian *fede* (faith) ring, which was similar, with the exception of the crown. Claddagh rings had high and low crowns. Men usually wore the high crown version. If a person was single, he or she wore the ring with the crown towards the palm. If married, the crown faced the nail; i.e. the ring's heart faced the heart of the wearer. If love did not last and the marriage dissolved, the ring was reversed. Dating from 1700 or earlier, the ring was also worn outside the Claddagh – especially in Connemara and on the Aran Islands.

SEVEN

BETWEEN THE JIGS AND THE REELS!

PATTERNS

It was worn by my father at the pattern,
race and fair,
When all the boys and pretty girls were
sure to be all there.
It was built a hundred years ago but divil
a worse for that,
A regular lady dazzler is me Auld
Skillara Hat.

The pattern (*patrún*, patron) was once a feature of almost every parish. As the name implies, it was a day to honour the local patron saint. Roman Catholic clergy celebrated Mass on the day in the local church or at the saint's shrine. The custom disappeared due to the Penal Laws. Instead, people began gathering at holy wells or church ruins. Many of the patterns held at wells coincided with the great festivals of *Lughnasa, Domhnach Chrom Dhubh*, or Garland Sunday. The venue, or 'pattern field', was constant and even the sale of land sometimes stipulated that the field must be given over for the event each year.

Fun and games followed the serious business of the day. Young women, dressed in finery, ogled men in their Sunday suits. Field sports included running, jumping, tossing sheaves or horseshoes, donkey or pony races and assorted gambling games. For children there were egg and spoon races, sack races and three-legged races (*see* Games and Pastimes, *below*). Hawkers inevitably turned up to trade their wares. Sometimes the event was also a 'holy fair', where trading took place in livestock, poultry, crops and home-produced dairy products. If the saint's feast day fell during harsh winter months, another day in summer substituted. Fiddlers and flautists, melodeon, *bodhrán* and pipe players encouraged the merrymakers to continue their revels into the night. In some districts the hospitality of the people who lived near the well was such that few bothered to bring food or drink with them on pattern day. Furthermore, there were always whorts (bilberries) or 'moonogues' (a speckled fruit, similar to crowberries, found in marshy ground) for the picking.

DANCING AND SINGING

In Connemara the word '*prinkum*' (soirée, 'hoolie', celebration) is sometimes used for a *céili* or house party. The word once described a form of *rinnce fada* (long dance) and also the cake dance which was a feature of folk life. This ritual varied from place to place but always involved an elaborately decorated cake and took place at a crossroads or near a drinking house. The proprietor sometimes provided the cake and placed it outdoors to keep his premises from being overcrowded. A young man and young woman, often called the 'hurling couple', led the dance, collecting money for the musicians as they did so. A number of theories exist about cake dances. One claims that the raised decorations included the signs of the zodiac (a type of Ouija-cake!).

In County Roscommon participants danced around a cake placed on an upturned churn dash stuck in the ground. In other locations the dance took place at patterns. One thing is common to all accounts, however: the best dancer took the cake. But if he did, the poor fellow also was obliged to treat everybody to a drink. On *Lá Féile Muire Mór* music, bargaining and dancing was enjoyed on Erris Head (*see* 8 September, 'Throughout the Year'). The couples who took the floor ('riz the dust' was an accurate description) at Erris were 'the Almighty best in the land' and he who took the cake there became really famous.

People still remember crossroads dances, and even revive them on occasions. Kilkenny folk still talk about 'the boords at Ballycallen' and its long dance called the High Gates. Ned's Cross in County Meath was a favourite venue also. Maypole dancing on 1 May was popular too.

To visit a house for a 'colloguing cup', for storytelling or chatting, singing or dancing was to *céilí* or participate in a 'kitchen racket'. It was the equivalent to the 'craic' that is 'ninety' at some parties today. At least one house in every district was a *céilí* house.

More organised events took place in homesteads, where hosts paid small sums to musicians. Sometimes, poor people co-hosted a 'joined *céilí*' or 'joined melodeon'. When wealthier homes held parties or dances, there was a 'scrap party' the day after, and domestic staff and friends attended to polish off the leftovers.

Under Irish hearths was a deep pit for holding the ashes, which continued under the large slab in front of the hearth known as *Leac na Teine* (the Fire Stone). The stone was reserved for the *fear a' tí* when there was dancing. He would clatter his feet on it and, because of the pit beneath, his dancing gave the greatest resonance. Liscannor stone from County Clare was recognised as best for the purpose.

In London, in 1897, the Gaelic League held its first public *céilí*, featuring Irish dancing, sets and singing. During the first half of the twentieth century, local newspapers in Ireland regularly advertised a 'Céilí and Old Time [Waltz]'. Today's *céilí* is likely to feature The Siege of Ennis, The Stack of Barley, The High Caul Cap, The Walls of Limerick. A *rinnce fada* of the seventh century would have been similar to today's dance called The Bridge of Athlone. Set dancing evolved from

Parisian quadrilles popular with soldiers returning from the Napoleonic Wars. The Cashel Set or the Corofin Set are still among the most popular. A whoop or yelp from a musician or dancer is customary as tempo mounts.

Raised dancing platforms were common for *feiseanna*, but a door made lubricious with soap often sufficed, and a dance was sometimes referred to as a 'Rattle-the-Hasp', the hasp being the latch that rattled to the dancers' steps. (The term also described a man who was edgy and flying around the farmyard.) As the competition became more intense, the dancing area was reduced and often ended in less than a square yard of space, marked out by twigs.

People attending traditional music sessions in public houses or in the open air nowadays might benefit from knowing some etiquette associated with live performances. True musicians become immersed in the *draiocht* (magic) of the notes and do not appreciate sudden intrusion by newcomers with a *bodhrán* or a guitar. Unrequested solo singing is also taboo. The oldest performer usually dictates the airs and their pace and rhythm. He may call upon a singer to perform and to be given 'a bit of hush'. When the song ends, the singer has the 'noble call'; that is, the right to call on someone else to sing. The company would take the singing seriously and there was always one person to admonish someone trying to join in by calling, 'One voice only, now!' The same person might offer some encouragement, like, 'Get under it, gossoon,' or criticism: 'Run outside and get an air for that.' *Sean nós* (old custom or style) is highly embellished and unaccompanied solo singing of traditional airs.

MUMMING

Mumming is still performed in parts of Ireland. It brings together a number of art forms, including drama, music, poetry and dancing. Performances once reflected some social reality, where protagonists faced each other with menace. A chorus of strawboys accompanied characters as diverse as Saint George, a golden-nosed Oliver Cromwell, Saint Denis, Prince George, Saint Patrick, Beelzebub, armed with frying pan and flail, a Doctor and a Priest. A 'wee devil' collected the money, but was also tossed about by the others. An old woman created fun too. Their antics were accompanied by verse. For example, the Doctor declared:

> *I can cure for a decent fee*
> *From ague or fever set you free.*
> *I cure by day, I cure by night*
> *And I can diagnose by sight ...*
> *I fixed a woman of ninety-eight*
> *Who fell off her ass and broke her pate.*

She thought it was a great disaster
But I mended her with my famous plaster.

The drama enacted by County Wexford mummers
had characters from Irish history and a sword dance.

GAMES AND PASTIMES

Gaelic Games

Irish mythology includes references to striking a
ball with a stick, and twelfth-century manuscripts
describe games like hurling and football. Hurling
was once played across parishes or townlands and
often featured complementary wrestling matches.
A 'crooky stick' pulled from a hedge served as a
camán (hurley). Rolled and greased cord provided
a ball. Later there came 'summer hurling' with a
broad stick and 'winter hurling' with a narrow one.
Although a fast and furious game, the wearing of
protective helmets is a comparatively recent
innovation.

Youths often played Gaelic football by kicking
an inflated pig's bladder into goals formed from
two ash plants and a string of binder twine.

At earlier GAA matches it was customary for
the crowd to stand facing the flag and sing the
hymn 'Faith of Our Fathers' and the national
anthem. The local bishop usually threw in the ball
for the start of play.

Women play camogie, a game similar to hurling, and handball is another GAA-controlled game. Ball-alleys were once a feature of village greens.

Rugby

Rugby has its own Irish traditions. The Garryowen is a high kick forward made famous by the Garryowen club in Limerick. It offers the kicker's team the chance to make ground and is customarily supported by shouts of 'Up,up,up!'

Soccer

In recent years customs have emerged in soccer. They include the hugging and kissing of a goal-scorer on the pitch, with a chorus 'Olé,Olé,Olé!' from the terraces, and the cramming of pubs for important away games.

Cricket

Cricket was once a popular game and almost every parish boasted at least one team. A public game between The Garrison and All Ireland was recorded in the Phoenix Park in 1792; the result was Garrison 240, All Ireland 76 and 70.

Bowling

The game of bowls (pronounced 'bowels') takes place mainly in County Cork but people in Counties Limerick, Waterford and Armagh also play. Contestants loft an iron ball or 'bullet', weighing 790 grams, along a road. The person who completes a set distance or course in the least number of throws wins. Betting between supporters of competitors is often heavy.

Horseracing

Ireland has a rich racing tradition and its classics are highly organised, but seashore and point-to-point races are popular old customs. 'Point to point' was an accurate description. Contestants raced across country from one point to another, usually church spires. The word 'steeplechase' was coined when, in 1752, contestants raced from Buttevant, County Cork, to St Leger, a distance of 7.2 kilometres.

Skittles

Skittles was once a popular crossroads team game that, in latter years, became confined to Ulster counties. Each player stood at a 'spud' and threw an oak or ash stick at five 'standers' which were placed within a circle five feet in diameter. The object was to clear all the standers out of the ring. Soaking sticks in water to give them weight was common.

Pitch-and-Toss

During the first half of the twentieth century men in navy Sunday suits congregated after Mass to play pitch-and-toss. Their local pitch-and-toss 'school' was at a crossroads or street corner. If the two pennies tossed in the air from a comb or a piece of wood came down heads or tails, the pitcher won. Other bets were laid on a pitcher landing his coin nearest a stone marker.

Horseshoe Throwing

'Ringing' a horseshoe on a peg in the ground at a set distance called for some skill. Men whiled away many hours competing with each other in this simple rural pastime.

Cards

Proprietors of bars or shebeens once refused to allow card-playing on their premises because they believed it was unlucky to play the game in public.

A card-player walked sunwise around a card table, stuck a crooked pin in the back of his lapel or kept his wife's wedding ring in his pocket for luck. In the home, a man never sat under a rafter while playing cards. That was unlucky. His wife sometimes sat behind him knitting, believing this would improve his chance of winning. If bad fortune persisted, turning his cap back to front or turning his coat inside out might help. Should a player stand up for some reason and knock his chair, nobody would use that chair for the rest of the card session. A man never lent money won at cards – that would pass on his luck to the recipient.

Innocent Pastimes

At patterns, bonfires and other celebratory
occasions assorted competitions and children's
games took place. These included gurning
(squeezing) through a horse's collar, three-legged
races, egg-and-spoon races (sometimes using
potatoes, for economy), wheelbarrow races,
grabbing the greased tail of a pig, jackstones, Kitty-
four-corners, blind man's buff, sack races and
hopping races, Dan, Dan, Thread the Needle, tig,
hide and seek and tip-cat.

Faction Fights

A celebrated faction fight at Garvagh in County
Derry is recorded in song:

Scarcely had he reeled around
Till he received a deadly wound.
His brogues riz up and his head went down
At the third tree up in Garvagh ...

Faction fights often involved hundreds of fighters.
Some groups bore names like Shanavests, Lane
Boys, Bootashees, Caravats, Lawlor-Black
Mulvihills, Pudding Lane Boys, Poleens,
Reaskawallaghs and many more. Fights were
between septs, baronies, parishes or namesakes to
establish which groups were the best. There were
serious injuries and even deaths. Fighters often

went into combat because of a minor insult, real or imagined, or just for the kick they got out of fighting. Women brought along bags of stones to the fights and there were renowned women of war too.

Cruel landlords sometimes lashed out at tenants with weighted riding crops. Following their example, faction fighters manufactured their 'loaded butts'. Pulling a stick (*maide, bata* or *cipín*) from a hedge and filling its knobbly end with lead or the like allowed it to pack a better wallop.

> I leathered him with my shillelagh
> For he trod on the tail of my coat.

Coat-trailing was a sort of dare, but was not, as the song suggests, a prelude to faction fighting. Most fights began with the 'wheeling' ritual, which involved a faction leader strutting up and down waving his *bata* and calling out something like: 'Caravats *abú*! Who dares strike a Caravat? Will a Shanavest dare?' He then made a sudden strike at an opponent.

COCKFIGHTING

Illegal cockfighting still takes place at dawn in secret venues throughout Ireland. Wearing steel spurs, the cocks fight in a ring. Heavy gambling takes place. Cock-throwing was another cruel pastime. The events occurred most often on Shrove

Tuesday and Ascension Thursday, and involved tethering a cock by the leg to a heavy stone while contestants flung a length of wood at it from a marked spot. The man who delivered the *coup de grâce* kept the bird as a spoil of victory.

HUNTING THE WREN

The custom of hunting the wren on Saint Stephen's Day (*see*, 26 December, 'Throughout the Year') was common to all Celtic nations. It arose from a theory that the bird gave away the hiding place of the first martyr by stirring in the ivy of the tree in which he was hiding. His pursuers looked up and saw Stephen. A quaint Irish story tells otherwise. It claims that the bird was despised after a foiled attack on Oliver Cromwell's sleeping troops. The tapping of a wren on a soldier's drum awakened Cromwell's men and they slaughtered the Irish. Holders of this theory buried a dead wren outside the door of an unpopular neighbour.

THEATRE

City theatres once had a custom of promenading: patrons walked along the aisles dressed in their finery and met and chatted with friends – even during the performance. Actresses were always in demand and young bucks often attempted to go backstage to meet them in their dressing rooms. Most theatres had an armed guard on the stage door to prevent unwanted entry. Audience interruptions were common and on one occasion a patron of Dublin's Smock Alley disliked the scenery so much that he walked onstage and hacked it to pieces with his sword. Servants and footmen of the nobility paid twopence to sit in the 'gods' (highest balcony) and fist fights between them were common.

Actors had their own set of customs and superstitions. They never whistled once they entered the stage door. Whistling in the dressing room was particularly serious. An offender was ejected and forced to turn around three times before he was re-admitted. Whistling in the auditorium was frowned upon too. If a shoe fell over on its side, an actor would try to get another pair, believing bad luck would follow if he wore the one that toppled. If a quick change necessitated the kicking off of a shoe, and if it landed upright, that was a good sign. The audience would accord a good welcome to the actor whose shoes squeaked on a first entrance.

The custom of an actor asking for a 'final round of applause' for a recently deceased colleague still takes place in theatres.

Companies liked playing in a theatre that had a cat – as long as it did not run across the stage during a performance. No matter how angry an actor became, he never kicked a cat.

Power failure or not, directors never lit three candles on a stage or in the dressing room. Custom stated that a quarrel among the cast would follow such an action.

Actors and actresses will not look into a mirror over somebody's shoulder. They will not call Shakespeare's famous play *Macbeth* by name; they refer to it as the 'Scottish play' and tell of a remarkable history of tragedy associated with the performance of this classic.

There are front-of-house customs too. Ushers vied to be the one to show the first customer to his or her seat because that was considered lucky. If the customer had a ticket for seat number thirteen, however, it augured badly for the run of the show. If an elderly person bought the first ticket, the show would have a successful long run. The opposite would happen if that customer were young.

At the close of the nineteenth century, the Midland Great Western Railway gave touring companies special concessions. They were allotted 'coupés handsomely lined with blue cloth' and were granted permission to carry double the amount of baggage usually allowed. They were also allowed to travel on Sundays, when the rail company could arrange direct journeys, thus saving them the trouble of having to change trains. These touring companies hired locals as extras.

Fit-up companies and circuses had their own

customs. An advance cart went from one town to the next over-night, with a leaking barrel of whitewash in the back. This dribbled onto the road and showed the main convoy the way next morning.

BANTER AND BLARNEY

Before big matches in Croke Park, Dalymount Park or Lansdowne Road, street vendors still call, 'Programme of the Match, Official Programme', and sell team favours. At Christmastime, Henry Street traders call, 'Last of the long decorations' or 'Would ya like a jumpin' monkey, Missus?'

Current social life in Ireland includes the practice of 'slagging' a person's weak points or tribulations. It is good-humoured and the target of the banter can always retaliate. A public form of the art may be observed at a modern boxing match. If the contestants are not mixing it enough, the audience, in derision, may lilt the 'Blue Danube' Waltz or call out: 'It's not a mortal sin to hit him.' At field games 'Put on a jersey, ref' is the admonishment for an unfair referee at field games.

Hundreds of tourists believe that they can acquire the Irish 'gift of the gab' by kissing the Blarney Stone in County Cork. The custom may have arisen because the MacCarthys of Muskerry kept a bardic school there – and nobody can utter *plámás* like a poet. More likely it arose when Cormac MacDermot MacCarthy promised Lord

Deputy Carew that he would renounce the
traditional system of electing chieftains and take
tenure of his lands from the Crown instead. Carew
kept reminding him to 'come in off his keeping'
but MacCarthy always postponed the event 'with
fair words and soft speech'. This continued until
Carew assured an impatient Queen Elizabeth that
MacCarthy was at last going to surrender his
rights. The queen retorted: 'This is all Blarney!
What he says, he never means.'

Blarney or good conversation – this is where
we came in. *Slán!*

EIGHT

'DEATH, WHERE IS THY STING-A-LING-A-LING?'

WAKES

In the distant past Irish people called the day a person died his 'third birthday'. Natural life began on the first birthday, supernatural life on the second, when he received the sacrament of Baptism. The third birthday gave eternal life.

When a person died, the senior family member stopped the clock in the house and did not set it in motion again until after the obsequies. As soon as people heard of a death in the district they suspended all work until after the funeral. Local women 'laid out the corpse' on a bed or on the kitchen table in the home of the deceased. They washed the body and dressed it in a white shroud (later, members of Third Orders wore their order's habit). Joining the corpse's hands, they entwined a set of rosary beads around the fingers and opened all windows to allow the soul to depart. Before pulling blinds or curtains, they lit the wake room with twelve candles standing in a basin of sand. (They replaced these when necessary but ensured that twelve kept burning until the body was removed from the house. Then they extinguished them one by one and gave the last one to be extinguished to the chief mourner.) If it was available, they also lit the baptismal candle of the deceased and placed it on a small altar set up beside the corpse. After a period of silence, it was time for the wake to begin.

Wakes were almost festive occasions, especially if they happened around a holiday or feast day, and lasted for three days and three nights. A huge gathering at a wake would be talked about for years. People regarded it as a farewell to a loved one and, believing in a better afterlife, they celebrated. The wake also helped close relatives through their grief.

'Like snuff at a wake' is an expression in praise of abundance. Near the door of a wake house each visiting mourner took a pinch of snuff or a clay pipe full of tobacco. Before sniffing or lighting up, the visitor said a prayer for the dead person and offered the relatives their condolences. In some parts of the country the family placed the saucer of snuff on the corpse. Because it did not rise and fall with the motion of breathing, it confirmed death.

Family pride demanded generous hospitality and so food and intoxicating drink were bounteous.

People believed that liveliness was important because crying over a corpse could give its soul a tormented afterlife. Wake amusements included cards and simple sport, like hiding a guest's cap and asking others to guess where it was. Telling ghost stories was popular too. There were almost two hundred recorded wake games with names like *An Déideadh Dhogha* (The Burning Toothache), Kissing the Goat, and *Gadaidhe Ruadh nagCappall* (The Red Thief of the Horses).

Should things get out of control, the host might place a candle in the corpse's hand because, according to tradition, that would make everybody fall asleep. Outside in the haggard, when the candles caused the atmosphere in the house to become stuffy, men passed the time knocking skittles, throwing horseshoes, lifting barrels, lofting turnips and playing leapfrog. Practical jokes were common too.

A member of the family always stayed in the room with the corpse and at midnight all would gather and each member of the family 'gave out' a decade of the Rosary. Usually, some local women began to *caoin* (keen, lament) after this. Keening before this stage in the proceedings could encourage evil spirits to take possession of the soul of the deceased. If the death had been sudden or the result of a tragedy, the keening did not begin until the third day, giving the soul of the deceased some time to converse with its Maker in silence. It was also necessary because two huge dogs slept near the place of Judgment and if awakened by wails, not even God had the power to prevent their grabbing the soul and devouring it!

When the three days had elapsed, undertakers or neighbours brought the coffin to the house and placed it on two chairs. Only the family remained in the room while the corpse was laid in the coffin. When the helpers closed the coffin and lifted it, a family member upturned each chair on its back, where it remained until the funeral cortège had begun to move away from the house. Likewise, he upturned the bed or table upon which the corpse had lain. These actions turned further death away from the family.

Family members and close family friends, three on each side, carried the coffin. If the journey was long, it was placed on a cart. Women were barred from sitting in a cart that had drawn a corpse to its burial place nor was a mare ever used to pull it. If a person met a funeral, he turned and walked some of the way with it. Should it be a man riding a white horse, he passed on, but one mourner always went back and forced the rider and mount to join the cortège for a few yards.

The funeral procession approached the graveyard from a direction that would take it over water. For this reason, some coastal families went as far as burying their dead on nearby islands. They laid the coffin on a large stone slab before bringing it across. If the corpse had been brought to the church and the route to the cemetery passed the deceased's home, the cortège stopped for a few moments. It also stopped at crossroads, where the mourners recited prayers. A funeral never took a short cut to the cemetery – to do so was considered an insult to the dead person. Nobody wore a new garment to a funeral, as it was unlucky.

If two funeral cortèges arrived at a cemetery together, one always remained outside until the other left. This caused distress among people who believed the second corpse would have the task of bringing water to every corpse in the cemetery until the next funeral.

Gravediggers would never open a family plot already holding remains on New Year's Day. Doing so would mean opening a grave every day during the year. Recalling the cross of Christ, gravediggers left their implements crossed above the open grave or else placed two crossed twigs at either end. When the coffin arrived, the bearers carried it three times around the crosses before lowering it into the grave. A member of the family threw the first bit of clay onto the coffin and the gravediggers completed the filling and again crossed their shovels on top. In parts of Kerry, after lowering the coffin, the gravedigger climbed into the grave and loosened its lid, in case the soul of the deceased had not yet parted.

To be last out of a cemetery after a funeral was unlucky and this sometimes caused a scramble. If someone lost an article in the cemetery, they would never go back to search for it. A woman's corpse buried in a man's cemetery would be ejected.

A county Kerry mother never attended the funeral of her first child. Where a family bonfire was customary on Saint John's Eve (23 June), it was cancelled if there had been a death in the family during the previous year. The recipient of a dead person's clothes wore them to Mass on three consecutive Sundays. If he were ill, he was obliged to send the clothes along in a bundle. No family member attended patterns or other celebratory events during the year following a bereavement. In some areas, each mourner laid a stone near where a man died. Nobody ever disturbed the resulting mound.

THE RECENT PAST
Some of the earlier customs survived into the recent past, when custom demanded 'black mourning' for a month and general mourning for a year. Men wore a black tie and a black cloth diamond on their right sleeve. Women dressed in black from head to toe, and widows remained in this garb for at least a month, but, more often, a year. They did not attend public functions or entertainments.

A sombrely clad undertaker in tails and silk hat walked before the hearse; if horse-drawn, the

horses wore black plumes when the deceased was
an adult and white for a child.

The practice of 'offerings' at a funeral was
widespread. The priest stood at the head of the
coffin as the head of each household filed past and
placed an offering on a plate. The status of the
deceased was assessed by the total amount
collected; the amount donated reflected on the
donor also. Households unable to send a
representative gave an envelope containing their
offering to a friend, who placed it on the plate
along with this own. Some unscrupulous people
would place a half-crown in an envelope and
thump out its impression before replacing it with a
shilling!

Householders along the funeral route pulled
blinds or drew curtains and closed shutters until
the cortège had passed by. If the cortège passed the
home or place of employment on the way to the
cemetery, it halted for a minute. After the burial,
sympathisers approached the family to offer
condolences.

On Good Friday, some people prostrated
themselves on graves of relatives and prayed for
them. It was also customary to take some earth
from a grave of a person who had been renowned
for holiness during life, and keep it in the home.

CURRENT CUSTOMS

Nowadays, a home wake is rare. Either at the morgue or funeral home, in the church or at the graveside, mourners line up, shake hands with the bereaved, say 'I'm sorry for your trouble', or utter some similar expression of sympathy. Before the body leaves the morgue or funeral home, they sprinkle it with holy water or make the Sign of the Cross on the forehead with their thumb. A bell tolls as the cortège leaves the church, occasionally led by a lone piper playing a lament. Close relatives and good friends like to walk behind the hearse or carry the coffin, if the journey to the cemetery is not too long. Parish cemeteries have a *listín*, or small corner, in which to bury unbaptised children who have died. This is known as the Plot of the Angels.

Many parishes still have a Cemetery Sunday, when relatives of the dead come home, often from abroad. They assemble for an organised prayer service in the cemetery. Before the Sunday, those at home tidy up their loved ones' graves; after the formal service, they often enjoy a family get-together.

GLOSSARY

bairín breac: barm brack

bean a' tí: woman of the house

besom: a broom usually made from heather

bodhrán: A tambourine type of drum used in traditional Irish music. Usually made from dried, stretched goatskin on a circular frame, it is held in one hand and beaten with the other hand and fingers or with a bone.

calp: Originally black Carboniferous limestone, later adopted to denote one of the lithological divisions of Carboniferous rocks. Nowadays the word is used to describe a local dark-coloured Dublin stone that is 95 per cent granite, while 4 per cent of the remainder is sandstone.

caubeen: (*caipín*) Cap. Usually an old battered one.

clúdóg: A set or hatching. A batch of about a dozen eggs.

craobh: branch

crios: belt

Crom Dubh: a pagan idol, worshipped particularly in Munster and Connaught

Cúchullain: Cullan's hound, sometimes called the Hound of Ulster. A great hero in Irish mythology, prominent in the epic *An Táin*.

dray: cart

drúchtín: (lit. a light dew or a white slug).
Although the Irish for a snail is *seilide*, in
reference to the custom, people used *drúchtín*.

fear a' tí: man of the house

feis: (pl: *feiseanna*, lit: festival) A traditional Irish
music and singing competition, usually held
outdoors except for major events.

flagger: a wildflower of the Iris strain found in
damp ground

GAA: Gaelic Athletic Association

gale day: a day on which rent instalment became
due

gríosach: hot ashes

haggard: area of a farmyard where hay and straw
are stored

JCKAS: Journal of County Kildare Archaeological
Society

lá: day

meitheal: A group of neighbours coming together
to help in major farming operations, like
harvesting, threshing or turf-cutting.

Penal Laws: anti-Catholic legislation of the
seventeenth century

piseóg: Superstition, charm or 'old wives' tale. Also,
pishogue, pishrogue.

plámás: flattery, soft talk

poc: male goat

poitín: (poteen) Illicit spirit; mountain dew.

Pooka: A common creature in Irish folklore.

Usually a dark phantom horse galloping on cloven hooves, representing the Devil. Sometimes it is a goat or donkey, which can contaminate water.

quarter day: A day on which tenancies begin or end, quarterly rents and other agreed payments become due.

seanchaí: story-teller

shebeen: (*síbín*) Speakeasy. Unlicensed drinking house.

sí gaoithe: fairy wind or whirlwind

slash-hook: A straight or slightly hooked blade on a handle used for cutting thick hedges.

sliothar: hurling ball

spailpíní: seasonal hired labourers

Tone, Theobald Wolfe: (1763–98) Co-founder of the United Irishmen who raised a small force in France to assist the 1798 Rebellion. His own arrival was late and he was arrested in Lough Swilly, County Donegal. He committed suicide in a Dublin prison.